Timothy Keller

Romans 8-16

In View of God's Mercy

● 7-Session Bible Study

Romans 8-16 For You

These studies are adapted from *Romans 8–16 For You*. If you are reading *Romans 8–16 For You* alongside this Good Book Guide, here is how the studies in this booklet link to the chapters of *Romans 8–16 For You*:

Study 1 > Ch 1
Study 2 > Ch 2-3
Study 3 > Ch 4-5
Study 4 > Ch 5-6
Study 5 > Ch 7-9
Study 6 > Ch 10
Study 7 > Ch 11-12

Find out more about *Romans 8–16 For You* at: www.thegoodbook.com/for-you

Romans 8–16: In View of God's Mercy
A Good Book Guide
© Timothy Keller/The Good Book Company, 2015.
This edition printed 2025.

Published by The Good Book Company

thegoodbook.com | thegoodbook.co.uk
thegoodbook.com.au | thegoodbook.co.nz

Unless indicated, all Scripture references are taken from the Holy Bible, New International Version. Copyright © 1973, 1978, 1984 by the International Bible Society. Used by permission.

Timothy Keller has asserted his right under the Copyright, Designs and Patents Act 1988 to be identified as author of this work.

All rights reserved. Except as may be permitted by the Copyright Act, no part of this publication may be reproduced in any form or by any means without prior permission from the publisher.

A CIP catalogue record for this book is available from the British Library.

Design by André Parker and Drew McCall

ISBN: 9781802541915 | JOB-008231 | Printed in India

Contents

Introduction 4
Why Study Romans 8 – 16? 5

1. The Life of the Spirit 7
   Romans 8:1-13

2. Glorious Adoption 13
   Romans 8:14-39

3. Sovereign Mercy 21
   Romans 9:1 – 10:4

4. The Gospel and Israel 29
   Romans 10:5 – 11:36

5. New Relationships 37
   Romans 12 – 13

6. The Weak and the Strong 43
   Romans 14:1 – 15:1

7. Ministry and Mission 49
   Romans 15 – 16

Leader's Guide 55

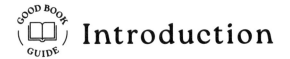

Introduction

One of the Bible writers described God's word as "a lamp for my feet, a light on my path" (Psalm 119:105, NIV). God gave us the Bible to tell us about who he is and what he wants for us. He speaks through it by his Spirit and lights our way through life.

That means that we need to look carefully at the Bible and uncover its meaning—but we also need to apply what we've discovered to our lives.

Good Book Guides are designed to help you do just that. The sessions in this book are interactive and easy to lead. They're perfect for use in groups or for personal study.

Let's take a look at what is included in each session.

Talkabout: Every session starts with an ice-breaker question, designed to get people talking around a subject that links to the Bible study.

Investigate: These questions help you explore what the passage is about.

Apply: These questions are designed to get you thinking practically: what does this Bible teaching mean for you and your church?

Explore More: These optional sections help you to go deeper or to explore another part of the Bible which connects with the main passage.

Getting Personal: These sections are a chance for personal reflection. Some groups may feel comfortable discussing these, but you may prefer to look at them quietly as individuals instead—or leave them out.

Pray: Here, you're invited to pray in the light of the truths and challenges you've seen in the study.

Each session is also designed to be easily split into two! Watch out for the **Apply** section that comes halfway through, and stop there if you haven't got time to do the whole thing in one go.

In the back of the book, you'll find a **Leader's Guide**, which provides helpful notes on every question, along with everything else that group leaders need in order to facilitate a great session and help the group uncover the riches of God's light-giving word.

Why Study Romans 8 – 16?

How does faith in the gospel of Christ actually lead to change in real life?

In view of God's mercy, how will we think, speak, and act?

Those are the questions Paul addresses in the second half of the book of Romans. At the heart of chapters 8 to 16 lies a key verse:

> "Therefore, I urge you brothers, *in view of God's mercy*, to offer your bodies as living sacrifices, holy and pleasing to God."
>
> (12:1, emphasis added)

The Christian life is lived with our gaze on God's mercy to us. Our eyes are fixed on the cross, where Christ died so that we need never fear condemnation by or separation from God.

And this, Paul says as he writes to the church in Rome in the middle of the first century, is to shape everything we are and do. The Christian life is a life of gratitude to our merciful Father. We live to please him by obeying him, even at cost or inconvenience.

How can we do this? In chapter 8, Paul will show us that it is by setting our mind on what the Spirit desires, as children of the Father.

How do we do this? In chapters 12 to 16, Paul will take us on a tour of our lives, showing how we live as grateful sacrifices in every facet of life.

The gospel makes a difference not only to our eternal future but to our present perspectives and priorities, attitudes and actions. These seven studies in the second half of this wonderful letter will show you why and how to live in view of God's mercy.

Carl Laferton
Editor

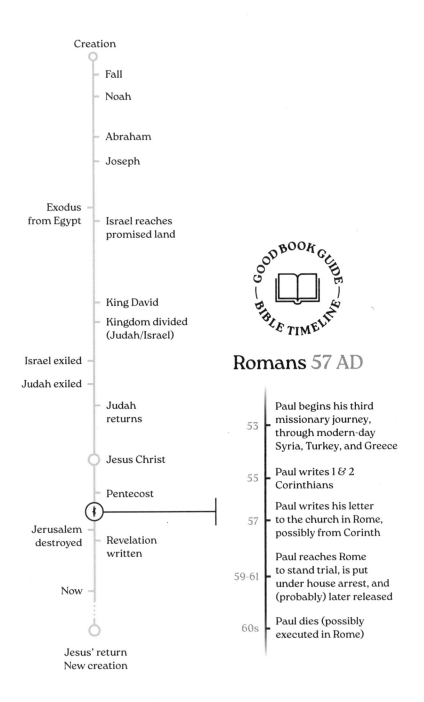

Romans 57 AD

- Creation
  - Fall
  - Noah
  - Abraham
  - Joseph
- Exodus from Egypt
  - Israel reaches promised land
  - King David
  - Kingdom divided (Judah/Israel)
- Israel exiled
- Judah exiled
  - Judah returns
  - Jesus Christ
  - Pentecost
- Jerusalem destroyed
  - Revelation written
- Now
- Jesus' return / New creation

53	Paul begins his third missionary journey, through modern-day Syria, Turkey, and Greece
55	Paul writes 1 & 2 Corinthians
57	Paul writes his letter to the church in Rome, possibly from Corinth
59-61	Paul reaches Rome to stand trial, is put under house arrest, and (probably) later released
60s	Paul dies (possibly executed in Rome)

1

The Life of the Spirit

Romans 8:1-13

Talkabout

1. What do you think about when you have nothing much to do?

- What do you think this says about you?

Investigate

📖 **Read Romans 8:1**

The first word of verse 1 is "Therefore." This reminds us that we are starting halfway through Paul's letter to the Romans.

2. Read the following verses to understand what Paul is saying in 8:1.
   - 1:18-21

- 2:1-3, 5

- 3:9-11

- 3:21-26

- 5:1-2

- 6:5-7

- 7:21-25

3. What does the phrase "no condemnation" mean? Put Romans 8:1 into your own words.

- Paul is saying there is "no condemnation" at all—not only no condemnation of our past, but of our present and our future too. Why is this important?

Getting Personal | OPTIONAL

If we forget that there can never be any condemnation for us if we are in Christ, what happens? We feel more guilt, unworthiness, and pain than we should. We're defensive when criticized; have a lack of confidence in prayer; and obey out of fear. But if we remember, we know we are accepted; we can handle disappointment and criticism; we pray confidently; we obey out of gratitude and love.

When do you find it easiest to live as though you are, or could be, condemned?

How will you remember that "there is now no condemnation"?

📖 Read Romans 8:1-4

DICTIONARY

The law (v 2): here, meaning "rule."
The law (v 3, 4): here, Paul is referring to God's law in the Old Testament.

Sinful nature or **flesh** (v 3): our natural selves, which desire to disobey God.
Sin offering (v 3): a sacrifice that pays the debt for people's sin.

4. What has the "Spirit of life" done for Paul, and for all Christians (v 2)?

5. What could the law (i.e. trying to obey God's commands) not do, and why (v 3)?

- How did God do it?

Apply

Verse 4 tells us that everything that Jesus went through—his incarnation, his death, and his resurrection—was all in order for us to live according to the righteous requirements of God's law, in the power of his Spirit.

6. How will this motivate us to live God's way?

Investigate

📖 **Read Romans 8:5-13**

> **DICTIONARY**
>
> **Righteousness** (v 10): right standing before God.

7. What do verses 5-8 tell us about people who…
   - "live according to the sinful nature"?

   - "live in accordance with the Spirit"?

8. What do verses 9-11 tell us about Christians?

9. How do people "die," and what is the way to "live" (v 13)?

- What does this look like in reality?

Apply

10. How can we make sure we have our "minds set on what the Spirit desires" (v 5)?

Explore More | OPTIONAL

📖 Read Colossians 3:1-14

- How do Paul's words here help us to know how to set our minds on spiritual things?
- How will doing so show itself in our thoughts and lives?

---

11. What motivations throughout the passage have there been to "put to death the misdeeds of the body" (v 13)?

- How can we motivate ourselves to do this?

- How can we encourage each other to do this?

Getting Personal | OPTIONAL

The 20th-century Archbishop of Canterbury William Temple once said, "Your religion is what you do with your solitude." Wherever your mind goes most naturally and freely when there is nothing else to distract it—that is what you really live for. Your life is shaped by whatever preoccupies your mind.

Where does your mind go most naturally? What does this say about you?

What truths from this passage will you consciously think about in your solitude this week?

Pray

Spend time praising God for the great truth that, in Christ, "there is now no condemnation."

Thank God for the gift of the Spirit in your life. Speak to him now about ways in which you find it difficult to "live in accordance with what the Spirit desires."

Finish your time of prayer by each reading a verse of your choice from this passage and praising God for the truths it contains.

2

Glorious Adoption

Romans 8:14-39

The Story So Far...

There is never any condemnation for the Christian; instead, we are free to live as the Spirit directs. We resist sin by setting our minds on the gospel.

Talkabout

1. If you could become a member of a famous family, which family would you choose, and why?

Investigate

📖 **Read Romans 8:14-17**

> **DICTIONARY**
>
> **Abba** (v 15): Daddy.
>
> **Testifies** (v 16): witnesses; tells the truth.

2. How does Paul describe the identity of those who are "led by the Spirit"—i.e. people with faith in Christ?

This is not something we automatically have because we are humans. It is something that is "received" (v 15), by faith. Paul is talking about divine adoption. In Roman society, a wealthy adult who had no heir for his estate would often adopt someone as his heir. If you were adopted, all your debts were paid for and canceled; you got a new name; you stood to inherit all your new father had; and you had new obligations to honor and please your father. All this lies behind the passage here.

3. What are the privileges of being an adopted son of God?
- v 15

- v 16

- v 17

Apply

Paul says that Christians are not given a "spirit that makes you a slave ... to fear," but rather "the Spirit of sonship" (v 15).

4. What difference does it make to us that we know God as a Father, not simply as a Master?

Getting Personal | OPTIONAL

"By him we cry, '*Abba*, Father'" (v 15).

How do you need this truth to…
- comfort you?
- excite you?
- change how you pray?

Investigate

📖 **Read Romans 8:18-25**

DICTIONARY

Consider (v 18): believe.
Firstfruits (v 23): the first batch of an incoming harvest—a foretaste of what is to come.
Redemption (v 23): freedom.

Hope (v 24): in the Bible, hope is not wishing something might happen, but rather, knowing with confidence that it will happen.

In verse 17, Paul says that God's family will share in their brother Jesus' sufferings, and that if we do, we will share in his glory. But is it worth it?

5. How does Paul answer that question in verse 18? How are his words stronger than simply saying, "Yes, it is"?

6. Why? What does Paul say is in store for…
- the creation?

- the children of God?

7. How should we be waiting for the day when we see our Father face to face?
   - v 23

   - v 25

Apply

8. When is it hardest to do these (i.e. your answers to question 7)? What difference would being eager and/or patient make at those moments?

Investigate

📖 **Read Romans 8:26-39**

DICTIONARY

Intercedes for (v 26): represents; speaks for.

Saints (v 27): holy ones, i.e. Christians.
Conformed to (v 29): changed into.

The Spirit will help us when we do not know how to pray (v 26-27). But Paul says there is one thing a Christian can always know.

9. What is it (v 28)?

- How does verse 29 help us understand what "the good" that God wants for his children is?

Explore More | OPTIONAL

- How do we see Paul living out what he says in Romans 8:28-29?
  - 2 Corinthians 12:7-9
  - Philippians 3:10-11

Getting Personal | OPTIONAL

Reflect on how God has been working for your good in…
- the good.
- the bad.
- your failings.

Now, think about how each of those circumstances could harden you toward God, or lead you to rely on him and become more Christ-like.

It is not as important to change our circumstances as it is to change our heart's attitude and stance toward them. How might you need to do this today?

---

10. What do each of the verbs in verses 29-30 mean, do you think?

- How do they give us confidence?

Apply

11. How do Paul's questions and answers in verses 31-39 help us when we…
    - are afraid (v 31)?

    - are unsure that we will keep going as Christians (v 32)?

    - feel guilty (v 33-34)?

    - worry about whether God loves us (v 35-39)?

12. How does this passage tell us…
    - who we are?

    - whether living with Jesus as Lord is worth it?

    - whether we might get lost on the way to our home with our heavenly Father?

Pray

Speak to your Abba now, asking the Spirit to help you pray. Use your answers to question 2 to prompt yourself to praise and thank him.

Speak to God about circumstances you are finding difficult right now. Ask him to be at work for your good in those things, as he promises to be. Pray that you would want to be conformed to Christ-likeness more than you want to change your circumstances.

3

Sovereign Mercy

Romans 9:1 – 10:4

The Story So Far…

There is never any condemnation for the Christian; instead, we are free to live as the Spirit directs. We resist sin by setting our minds on the gospel.

God has adopted Christians as his children, with wonderful privileges. He will bring us into his renewed creation, and he works for our good in all things.

Talkabout

1. What does the idea of God's "election" mean to you? How do you feel when you think about it?

Investigate

📖 **Read Romans 9:1-5**

DICTIONARY

Cursed (v 3): by God.
Covenants (v 4): the binding promises that God made to his people in the Old Testament.

Patriarchs (v 5): the first ancestors of Israel—Abraham, Isaac, and Jacob.

---

2. How does Paul feel about the fact that most of his fellow Jews have rejected Jesus as their King and Savior?

Getting Personal | OPTIONAL

Paul is saying, *I would give up all the benefits of knowing Christ that I have been speaking of in Romans 1 – 8, if somehow that meant my relatives were saved.*

How does the emotion of Paul's words in 9:1-5 move and challenge you?

Is there someone you need to be in anguish about, praying for, and actively trying to share the gospel with?

Romans 8 ends in a tremendous crescendo of confidence. Christians have been foreknown and predestined for eternal life; they will get there (v 30). Nothing can "separate us from the love of God that is in Christ Jesus our Lord" (v 39).

But Paul now imagines someone coming and saying, *Hold on, Paul! You say that when God calls someone, he always brings them all the way home. But what about the Jews? God promised their ancestor Abraham that he would have an heir, and that his descendants would be blessed (Genesis 12:1-3; 15:1-6). Yet his descendants, the Jews, have rejected Jesus as the Christ. So maybe God's calling and purpose can be rejected?*

Paul's answer takes us deep into who God is and how he works.

📖 Read Romans 9:6-18

DICTIONARY

Offspring (v 7): here, it means children who inherit God's promises.
Reckoned (v 7): considered, counted.
Election (v 11): choosing.

Loved and **hated** (v 13): this is part of a Hebrew saying, meaning one is preferred, the other not (rather than literally hated).

Pharaoh (v 17): Paul is referring to the Egyptian ruler at the time God freed Israel from slavery in Egypt.

Hardens (v 18): makes someone rebellious against God.

Paul says that God's word—his promise to save and bless Abraham's descendants—has not failed, even though most members of the nation of Israel have rejected Jesus as Lord (v 6).

3. Why not (v 6, 8)?

- Read Genesis 16:1-4a, 15-16; 17:15-22. How do we see the truth of Romans 9:6 in what happened to Abraham's children, Isaac and Ishmael?

So now the question is: why is it that some of Abraham's descendants love God and are true to Israel, and others do not and are not? To answer this, Paul considers Isaac's twin sons, Esau (the elder son) and Jacob. Just like Isaac and Ishmael, one inherited God's promise of blessing; the other did not.

4. What did God tell Rebekah about her twins (v 12)?

- What reasons for God blessing Jacob and not Esau does Paul rule out (v 11, 12)?

- Is any positive reason given for God's election of Jacob? What is it?

So now the question is: is God unjust? (v 14), because he chooses some (like Jacob) and not others (like Esau). Paul now moves on through Israel's history to the time of the Exodus—the time of Moses and Pharaoh.

5. On whom does God have mercy (v 15)?

- What does salvation therefore not depend on (v 16)?

Mercy, by definition, is undeserved. It is not owed to anyone. To say that having mercy on someone but not everyone is "unfair" is to say that it is owed to all. But then it would not be mercy—it would be something that had been earned. Since God doesn't owe salvation to anyone, he is free to give it to all, to some, or to none.

6. How does this help us to think through whether God is being unjust to choose some and not others?

Moses was someone God chose to give his mercy to. Pharaoh was someone he chose to harden; he did not receive mercy (v 17-18). To understand what is going on here, we need to head back to the Exodus account.

7. Read Exodus 4:21; 7:3; 10:1. Who hardened Pharaoh's heart?

- Read Exodus 8:15, 19; 9:7, 17, 27. Who hardened Pharaoh's heart?

All these statements are true! Paul has already spoken about this in Romans 1:24—people's hearts rejected God, and "therefore God gave them over" to their decision to reject him. God's hardening of Pharaoh's heart was "giving him up" to his own stubbornness. God gave Pharaoh what he chose—a hard heart.

The teaching is that God hardens those he wants to harden. And all those whom he hardens want to be hardened.

📖 Read Romans 9:19-29

DICTIONARY

Wrath (v 22): God's right anger at sin.
Gentiles (v 24): non-Jews.
Remnant (v 27): a very small part of a much greater whole.

Sodom and **Gomorrah** (v 29): two towns destroyed by God's judgment on their sin (see Genesis 19).

---

8. What are we reminded of in verses 19-21 about...
   - God?

   - ourselves?

Apply

9. How does the teaching of verses 1-29…
   - help us to worship God?

   - humble us?

   - make us hopeful for non-Christians?

   - give us confidence that we will reach heaven?

Investigate

📖 **Read Romans 9:30 – 10:4**

> **DICTIONARY**
>
> **Zion** (9:33): another name for Jerusalem, Israel's capital.
>
> **Zealous for** (10:2): passionate about.

10. Israel did not attain righteousness—they had not ended up being in right relationship with God. Why not (9:30 – 10:3)?

- What does verse 4 say is the way in which God has made it possible to be right with him?

Apply

11. Who is responsible for someone being saved?

- Who is responsible for someone not being saved?

12. How would you use Romans 9 to explain to a Christian friend (in as simple a way as you can!)…
    - what we mean by God's election?

- why it is good news for them?

Getting Personal | OPTIONAL

God's election means that "those who go to heaven have no one to praise but Jesus Christ" (D. James Kennedy).

How will this truth shape your thoughts and your prayers this week?

Pray

How has this passage encouraged you about who God is? Turn your answers into prayers of praise.

How has this passage challenged or troubled you? Take time to speak to God about these things now.

How has this passage encouraged you to pray for non-Christian family or friends? Spend time now asking God to have mercy on them.

4

The Gospel and Israel

Romans 10:5 – 11:36

The Story So Far...

There is never any condemnation for the Christian; instead, we are free to live as the Spirit directs. We resist sin by setting our minds on the gospel.

God has adopted Christians as his children, with wonderful privileges. He will bring us into his renewed creation, and he works for our good in all things.

God saves sinners. He chooses those he will show undeserved mercy to. People are responsible for their sin and rejection of the gospel.

Talkabout

1. Are there people or groups of people who, deep down, you think will never become Christians? Why do you think that?

Investigate

📖 **Read Romans 10:5-21**

DICTIONARY

Confess or **declare** (v 9): say what you believe is true.

Justified (v 10): declared not guilty, completely innocent.
Obstinate (v 21): stubborn, inflexible.

---

2. How does Moses say someone can be saved, in verse 5?

- What is the problem with seeking to be saved in this way?

- What does he say about a different way to be saved in verse 8?

- What does Paul say more specifically about this different way, now that Jesus has lived, died, and risen (v 9-13)?

3. What should the truths of verses 9-13 lead believers to do (v 14-15)? Why?

Getting Personal | OPTIONAL

God has sent us with the message of salvation. He may send us overseas, into the pulpit, or across the street to our neighbor. But ours are the beautiful feet, bringing good news (v 15).

Do you count it a privilege to be part of the way God saves people?

How could you have "beautiful feet," sharing good news this week?

Explore More | OPTIONAL

In verses 16-21, Paul returns to his original question: why haven't the Jews believed?

- What possibilities does he raise, and how does he answer them?
  - v 18
  - v 19-20
- What is the right answer, in verse 21?

Read Romans 11:1-16

> **DICTIONARY**
>
> **Baal** (v 4): a false god.
> **Grace** (v 5): undeserved kindness.
> **Transgression** (v 11): sin.
>
> **Apostle** (v 13): Christ's chosen messenger, who is sent with Christ's authority.
> **Reconciliation** (v 15): bringing back into friendship.

In verse 1, Paul says that God has not rejected his ancient people, Israel.

4. What evidence is there that God hasn't rejected them:
   - in the present (v 1)?

- from the past history of Israel (v 2-6)?

5. What has happened because of Israel's "transgression" (that is, their rejection of the gospel, v 11-12)?

- What effect does Gentile conversion have on Israel, and how does this affect Paul's ministry (v 11, 13-14)?

Paul is setting out three stages that Israel will go through with regard to the gospel of Jesus:
- Rejection, leading to the gospel being preached to the Gentiles (v 11-12).
- Envy that the Gentiles have been blessed by God, and they haven't, so some Jews repent (v 13-14).
- A future stage, when a large number of Jews accept Christ (v 15—Paul will go into more detail on this in verses 25-27).

Apply

Paul is "talking to you Gentiles" (v 13)—to mainly non-Jewish churches.

6. If your church is largely non-Jewish, are you a community that is living out the fulfillment of what God called Old Testament Israel to be? How? And how could you do this more?

- Would a devout Jew look at your church and be aroused to envy, so that they give the gospel a hearing?

Getting Personal | OPTIONAL

If the Jews had not stumbled beyond recovery (v 11), no one has.

Are there people that you think are beyond God's reach—that he has given up on? How will you undermine this attitude?

Would someone looking at your life envy the blessings you have and enjoy? Would they want to know what you have, which they don't?

Investigate

📖 **Read Romans 11:17-32**

> **DICTIONARY**
>
> **Grafted in** (v 17): process where a shoot from one plant is attached to, and draws food (sap) from, the root of another.

In this image, the olive tree is the people of God. Natural branches are Israel; wild branches are Gentiles.

7. What is Paul wanting the Gentile Christians to do or not do?
   - v 18-21

   - v 22

- v 23-24—what should they believe?

8. How does Paul say God views Israel (v 28)?

Apply

9. How should this shape our view of Jewish non-Christians?

- What practical difference should it make to you as a church and as individuals?

Investigate

📖 **Read Romans 11:33-36**

10. What is Paul praising God for here?

11. Why is it significant that this outbreak of spontaneous worship comes at the end of chapters 9 – 11?

Apply

12. Reread 9:1-5. Putting these verses alongside 11:33-36, what effect does Paul's knowledge of God's sovereign election of his people have on him?

- How can this shape our own reaction to the truths of Romans 9 – 11?

Getting Personal | OPTIONAL

Romans 11:33-36 shows us that our praise of God is built on the truth about God; that there should be no study of truth without praise; and that we do not need to understand everything about God and his plans in order for us to praise him.

What do you need to think about and wrestle with, having read chapters 9 – 11?

How will you make sure you are praising God even as you grapple with these truths?

Pray

Thank God for…

Confess…

Ask for help with…

5

New Relationships

Romans 12 – 13

The Story So Far...

God has adopted Christians as his children, with wonderful privileges. He will bring us into his renewed creation, and he works for our good in all things.

God saves sinners. He chooses those he will show undeserved mercy to. People are responsible for their sin and rejection of the gospel.

God has planned to save Jews and non-Jews; the right response to his sovereign plan of election is to praise his wisdom and power.

Talkabout

1. If you had to sum up the Christian's approach to life in a sentence, what would you say?

Investigate

📖 **Read Romans 12:1-2**

> **DICTIONARY**
>
> **Spiritual** (v 1): can also be translated "rational" or "logical."

2. What does Paul "urge [his] brothers"—fellow Christians—to do? What does each mean?
   - v 1

   - v 2

3. What motivation does Paul give in these verses for the hard work of Christian living?

Apply

4. How do we worship Christ? Why is this both exciting and challenging?

Investigate

📖 **Read Romans 12:3-8**

DICTIONARY

Sober (v 3): careful.
Function (v 4): role, job.

Prophesying (v 6): in this context, it seems to mean preaching.

"The measure of faith" does not mean "amount of faith" but rather "standard of faith." Paul is talking about the fact that all Christians know they needed saving by Christ, and have been saved by Christ. None of us deserve to be loved by God, yet all of us are completely loved by him.

5. How does this help us understand what it means to think of ourselves "with sober judgment" (v 3)?

6. How else should we view ourselves (v 5-6a)?

- What should we do with what God has given us (v 6b-8)?

📖 **Read Romans 12:9-21**

> **DICTIONARY**
>
> **Sincere** (v 9): genuine, real.
> **Bless** (v 14): seek to do good to.
> **Conceited** (v 16): hungry for self-glory.

7. How do these verses show us what it means to be a "living sacrifice" in our relationships…
   - within the church (v 9-16)?

   - toward those who persecute the church (v 17-21)?

📖 **Read Romans 13:1-7**

8. What do these verses show us about how we can please God in our relationships with our state?

Explore More | OPTIONAL

Is Paul saying that the Christian must always submit to the state in every situation, no matter what the state commands?

📖 **Read Matthew 22:21**

- In Romans 13:7, Paul is echoing Jesus' words here. What is Jesus saying about what we should give to "Caesar" (the state), and what we should not?

Remember, the state is "God's servant" (Romans 13:4). It is not God's master, and does not deserve our primary allegiance or submission. We worship God, not the states God has established.

📖 **Read Exodus 1:17; Daniel 3:4-6; 6:7; Acts 5:29**

- What do these Bible passages show us about the limits of the Christian's duty to submit to the state?

📖 **Read Romans 13:8-14**

DICTIONARY

Debauchery (v 13): excessive indulgence.

Dissension (v 13): arguing.
Gratify (v 14): satisfy, please.

---

9. What do verses 8-10 tell us about how we can truly love those around us?

- Why will this sometimes be unpopular with those we are trying to love?

10. What perspective should Christians have, and what difference will that perspective make (v 11-14)?

Apply

11. How, specifically, can you as individuals live more sacrificially this week...
    - toward other members of your church?

    - toward members of your community?

    - in your relationships with your state/government?

12. How can we encourage each other to live this way, even (or especially) when it is hard?

Pray

As a group, hold God's mercy at the cross in your view and praise him for what he achieved for you there.

Pray about your attitude toward…

- *yourselves.*
- *your church.*
- *your state and society.*

6

The Weak and the Strong

Romans 14:1 – 15:1

The Story So Far...

God saves sinners. He chooses those he will show undeserved mercy to. People are responsible for their sin and rejection of the gospel.

God has planned to save Jews and non-Jews; the right response to his sovereign plan of election is to praise his wisdom and power.

Because of God's mercy for us, we live a life of grateful sacrifice; this changes how we view ourselves, love our church, and live in our society.

Talkabout

1. What causes avoidable disagreement and division in churches?

Investigate

In Romans 1 – 11 Paul has explained the gospel: we are justified in God's sight by grace alone through faith alone because of Christ alone. If we fully understand the gospel (chapters 1 – 5) and experience the gospel (chapters 6 – 8), the result will be a life of grateful, joyous love.

In chapters 12 – 13, Paul has described this life of love, and how it transforms our relationships. Now, in chapter 14, he applies all he has been saying to a very specific case—a particular problem within the Roman congregation.

📖 **Read Romans 14:1 – 15:1**

DICTIONARY

Abstains (14:6): does not take part.

Mutual edification (v 19): everyone being built up and encouraged.

Paul is speaking to two groups in the church—the "weak" and the "strong."

2. What are the differences of opinion between them?
   - v 2-3

   - v 5

   - v 14, 20

   - v 21

3. How does this help us to understand what Paul means by "weak" and "strong"?

Explore More | OPTIONAL

It is interesting to compare this dispute with the one that had occurred in the Corinthian church.

📖 Read 1 Corinthians 8:1-13

- What was the issue among the Christians in Corinth?
- What were the "weak" worried about, and what did the "strong" understand?
- So how are the weak and the strong the other way around from in the Roman church?

4. How do the weak and the strong tend to view each other (v 3)?

Verses 3b-12 are mainly Paul's critique of the attitude of the weak, while verses 13b-21 are mainly addressing the strong.

5. What does Paul tell the weak that they are forgetting when they condemn a Christian who does something they consider forbidden?
- v 1b

- v 3b

- v 4

- v 5-8

- v 10-12

Apply

6. If and when we find ourselves judging another Christian's behavior, what has Paul taught us to think and do?

Getting Personal | OPTIONAL

Do you tend to want to rule all matters as being disputable; or no matter as being disputable?

Can you see any area in which you may be a weaker believer (to do so takes great self-awareness!)? If so, what might you be in danger of forgetting? How will you check your own position humbly; and how do you need to view those who disagree with what you believe on this point?

Investigate

7. What should the priority of a strong believer be (v 13)?

Paul uses the issue of eating meat to explain what he means. He is a "strong" believer—he knows no meat is unclean. He is free to eat whatever he wants. But he won't, and neither should the strong Roman Christians.

8. Why not (v 14-21)?

Paul has pointed out that there will be times when a Christian's conscience tells them not to do something, even though it would not go against God's word to do that thing.

9. What would be the problem with that Christian acting in that way, even though it is not wrong?

10. How does 15:1 sum up what a strong Christian's priority should be?

Apply

11. If and when another Christian thinks of as wrong something that we know we are free to do, what has Paul taught us to think and do?

12. What are the "disputable matters" in your church, where Paul's words here need to be applied, whether we're "weak" or "strong"?

- How could the weak and strong get it wrong in those areas?

Getting Personal | OPTIONAL

Are you a "strong" Christian when it comes to an issue that people disagree over within your church?

What would it look like for you to restrict your freedom to support a weaker believer, rather than use it for your own pleasure or comfort? How will you use the gospel to motivate yourself to love your weaker brothers or sisters?

Pray

Ask God to show you any ways in which you are "weak" believers. Confess any condemning attitudes you have had toward fellow Christians.

Ask God to help you to be a loving stronger believer whenever necessary. Speak to him about ways in which you need his help to use your freedoms to build up other Christians.

Pray for your church, that you would be united in the gospel, and godly when dealing with disputable matters.

7

Ministry and Mission

Romans 15 - 16

The Story So Far...

God has planned to save Jews and non-Jews; the right response to his sovereign plan of election is to praise his wisdom and power.

Because of God's mercy for us, we live a life of grateful sacrifice; this changes how we view ourselves, love our church, and live in our society.

We should not judge other Christians who do what we do not; and we should be considerate of those who do not do what we know we're free to do.

Talkabout

1. What do you think effective gospel ministry involves?

Investigate

📖 **Read Romans 15:1-13**

2. What ethical principle is laid down in verses 1-2?

- In what way is Jesus the great example of living this way (v 3)?

3. What do verses 3-4 teach us about the role that Scripture should have in our lives and churches?

4. In verses 5-13, Paul is talking about the unique unity churches have. What do verses 5-7 tell us about how Christian unity is formed?

Apply

5. How might the principle of verses 1-2 apply to your...
   - finances?

   - relationships?

   - choice of where to live?

Getting Personal | OPTIONAL

The principle of Romans 15:1 is sweeping because it applies in every area of life, to everyone that we meet.

How does it need to apply specifically to you? Is there anything you need to change, or start doing?

As ever in Paul's ministry and the book of Romans, the motivation and example for how we should live is Jesus Christ.

How will you use the gospel to prompt and shape your life to be one of serving others rather than pleasing yourself?

Investigate

📖 **Read Romans 15:14-24**

> **DICTIONARY**
>
> **Priestly duty** (v 16): as a priest presented offerings to God, so Paul presents Gentiles who have become Christians.
>
> **Sanctified** (v 16): made pure.
> **Illyricum** (v 19): the Balkans area of south-east Europe.

6. What do we learn about Paul's ministry of evangelism here?

- What applies to all Christians today, do you think?

Explore More | OPTIONAL

📖 **Read 1 Thessalonians 2:1-12**

- From this passage, what does effective evangelism and church leadership involve?
- What motivates this kind of whole-life, sacrificial ministry (v 4, 6)?

Investigate

📖 **Read Romans 15:23-33**

DICTIONARY

Macedonia and **Achaia** (v 26): two areas of modern-day Greece.

---

7. Paul was called to be a church-planting missionary. Why is it striking that he found time to raise money for, and deliver money to, the poverty-stricken churches around Jerusalem?

   - How does Paul motivate the Roman Christians to give?

8. How can the Christians in Rome join Paul in his struggles (v 30)? Why is this exciting?

📖 **Read Romans 16:1-24**

DICTIONARY

Commend (v 1): praise.

Apostles (v 7): here, Paul simply means "sent ones" i.e. missionaries (rather than those men chosen by Christ to preach with his authority).

9. Verses 1-23 give us some glimpses into the life of the early churches. What do they suggest to us about…
   - the ministry of women?

   - the diversity of the church?

   - the structure of the church?

   - the dangers to the church?

Apply

10. From these two chapters, what are the various ministries a church should be involved in?

    - Evaluate your own congregation and yourself individually in light of what you've seen.

Investigate

📖 **Read Romans 16:25-27**

11. These are the final words of this wonderful letter. How do they sum up several of its main themes?

Apply

12. Think back over your time in Romans 8 – 16 over the last seven sessions. Pick one encouragement the Lord has been giving you as an individual, and to your church, through this part of his word.

- Pick one challenge you feel the Lord has been posing to you, and your church.

Getting Personal | OPTIONAL

How has the Spirit been changing you as you have been thrilled and challenged from the second half of the book of Romans?

How do you need to ask the Spirit to keep changing you?

Pray

Share your answers to question 12, and (if you are happy to) the Getting Personal section above, and use these as the basis for your prayers together.

Romans 8-16

In View of God's Mercy

LEADER'S GUIDE

Leader's Guide: Introduction

This Leader's Guide includes guidance for every question. It will provide background information and help you if you get stuck. For each session, you'll also find the following:

The Big Idea: The main point of the session, in brief. This is what you should be aiming to have fixed in people's minds by the end of the session!

Summary: An overview of the passage you're reading together.

Optional Extra: Usually this is an introductory activity that ties in with the main theme of the Bible study and is designed to break the ice at the beginning of a session. Or it may be a "homework project" that people can tackle during the week.

Occasionally the Leader's Guide includes an extra follow-up question, printed in *italics*. This doesn't appear in the main study guide but could be a useful add-on to help your group get to the answer or go deeper.

Here are a few key principles to bear in mind as you prepare to lead:

- Don't just read out the answers from the Leader's Guide. Ideally, you want the group to discover these answers from the Bible for themselves.

- Keep drawing people back to the passage you're studying. People may come up with answers based on their experiences or on teaching they've heard in the past, but the point of this study is to listen to God's word itself—so keep directing your group to look at the text.

- Make sure everyone finishes the session knowing how the passage is relevant for them. We do Bible study so that our lives can be changed by what we hear from God's word. So, **Apply** questions aren't just an add-on—they're a vital part of the session.

Finally, remember that your group is unique! You should feel free to use this Good Book Guide in a way that works for them. If they're a quiet bunch, you might want to spend longer on the **Talkabout** question. If they love to get creative, try using mind-mapping or doodling to kick-start some of your discussions. If your time is limited, you can choose to skip **Explore More** or split the whole session into two. Adapt the material in whatever way you think will help your group get the most out of God's word.

1

The Life of the Spirit
Romans 8:1-13

The Big Idea
There is never condemnation for the Christian; instead, we're free to live as the Spirit directs. We do this by setting our minds on the truths of the gospel.

Summary
In Romans 7, Paul has showed that Christians still wrestle with remaining, indwelling sin. We do not do what we want to do. In chapter 8, Paul shows how God's Son has given us life—that, despite our ongoing sin, there is not and can never be condemnation from God for those who are in Christ. Then he goes on to show how to live according to the Spirit. The way to defeat sin is to live by the Spirit, and we do this by setting our minds on him—letting the things of the Spirit, i.e. the gospel, be what controls our thoughts (v 5).

This study begins (in question 2) by looking back over the first half of the book of Romans, so that your group understand what Paul has already said about the gospel. If you are using this guide straight after studying the first seven chapters, you could choose to leave out question 2.

Optional Extra
Before the study, ask each member to take a section of Romans 1 – 7 (split it into enough parts for each member of your group to have one part each), and then summarize at the start of the session what Paul teaches there about God, and about the gospel. You could encourage them to read the relevant section in *Romans 1–7 For You* or John Stott's Romans commentary in *The Bible Speaks Today* series.

Guidance for Questions

1. **What do you think about when you have nothing much to do?**
   - **What do you think this says about you?**

   There is no right or wrong answer to the first part of this question. The second part encourages people to realize that where our minds naturally go when we have nothing else to do suggests something of what our priorities are, and where our greatest joys lie. Question 10 and the final Getting Personal pick up on these questions.

2. **Read the following verses to understand what Paul is saying in 8:1.**

   The aim of this question is to summarize the teaching of Romans 1 – 7. So do not allow your group to spend too long discussing the details of each passage—the point is to see the main thrust of Paul's teaching in each section. If you need to save

time, you could look just at the first four passages.

- **1:18-21**
  God's wrath—his settled, right anger—is being poured out on people who suppress the truth about him, and worship other things instead.

- **2:1-3, 5**
  People who consider themselves "better" and pass judgment on those described in chapter 1—that is, the "religious"—are no better, because they rebel against God too. They don't think they need to ask for his mercy (repent, v 5)—so they face his wrath.

- **3:9-11**
  No one is "righteous"—i.e. no one is in right relationship with God. Naturally, no one even understands or seeks God.

- **3:21-26**
  NOTE: You may need to explain some of the words used in this passage:
  - Law = God's commands and standards
  - Justified = found not guilty, without a stain on their reputation
  - Redemption = freedom that is bought at a price
  - Sacrifice of atonement = literally "propitiation" i.e. to turn aside wrath

  God has made unrighteous people righteous—has found sinful people innocent—by sending his Son to die to take the punishment of his wrath on sin. So God is just—he has punished sin—and he is the one who justifies sinners, bringing them into right standing with him.

- **5:1-2**
  Because we are justified, we are at peace with God (instead of his enemies); we are friends with God—we have full access to him; and we know that we will one day be in glory with God, in his perfect presence.

- **6:5-7**
  Faith unites us with Jesus, so that his death is our death and we will be resurrected just as he was. Our sinful self died when Jesus died. So we are freed from sin—we can sin, but we no longer have to sin.

- **7:21-25**
  We are, however, still sinful. So we don't obey God as we want to in our "inner being." We go on needing to be rescued by Jesus.

3. What does the phrase "no condemnation" mean? Put Romans 8:1 into your own words.

It means to be free from any liability or penalty; that no one can find you guilty of any charge; that you don't need to fear any prosecution or punishment. So a paraphrase of 8:1 will be something like: *Anyone who has faith in Christ Jesus never, ever needs to fear any charge or punishment from God.*

- **Paul is saying there is "no condemnation" at all—not only no condemnation of our past, but of** our present and our future, too. Why is this important?

Many think that a Christian is only temporarily out from under God's condemnation. If we confess our sin then we're forgiven, as long as we don't sin again; but when we do, we're back under condemnation until we confess again. This would mean that Christians are constantly moving back and forth, in and out of condemnation, in and out of being loved and accepted by God. But in fact, Paul is saying that the moment we come into Christ—put our faith in his death for us—condemnation is gone for ever. Our performance, good or bad, is irrelevant—because we are in Christ, there can never be any charge against us, and there is nothing but acceptance and welcome for us.

4. **What has the "Spirit of life" done for Paul, and for all Christians (v 2)?**
"Set [us] free from the law of sin and death." "Law" here means a "driving force"—the thing that dominates us. (You might like to explain this to your group before they try to answer the question.) So in verse 1, we discover we are delivered from the condemnation of sin; verse 2 says we are no longer under the power of sin. This does not mean we do not sin, but it does mean that we are no longer under its power: we never have to sin.

5. **What could the law (i.e. trying to obey God's commands) not do, and why (v 3)?**
Remember, verse 3 follows the great declarations of verses 1-2. So the law—that is, following God's commands—does not bring us into a state of no condemnation, nor does it give us the ability to resist sin. It is powerless because of our sinful nature. We sin; and therefore we cannot keep the law, and so it cannot save. Because we are sinners, knowing the law actually increases the power of sin, rather than negating it (see 7:7-8).

- **How did God do it?**
  - He sent his Son to become a human ("in the likeness of sinful man") and to become a "sin offering"—to be the way that the debt incurred by our sinfulness is paid, at the cross.
  - Because of his Son's work, we can now have his Spirit (v 4), who empowers us to meet the "righteous requirements of the law." God sent his Son so that he could send his Spirit to wipe out sin in our lives.

- *OPTIONAL (if your group is struggling with this second aspect): One of the achievements of the cross is that Christians can now have God's Spirit living in them. What are those who live according to the Spirit now able to do (v 4)?*

- *OPTIONAL: What does this show was one of the achievements of God's actions in sending his Son?*

6. **How will this motivate us to live God's way?**
Whenever we sin, we act to frustrate the aim and purpose of the entire life, death, and ministry of Jesus Christ.

If this doesn't work as an incentive for a holy life, nothing will.

7. What do verses 5-8 tell us about people who...

- **"live according to the sinful nature"?**
  - They have their minds set on what that nature desires (v 5)—their thinking is dominated by their own desires.
  - Their mind "is death" (v 6). This is not simply, or even primarily, meaning the future death of condemnation from God; Paul says it *is* death. He is referring to the brokenness and sense of dislocation that is experienced in this life by those whose lives are driven by their sinful desires. You could ask your group, "Why does Paul say this way of life 'is' death, not 'will be' death? What point is he trying to make about the life of the sinful nature now?"
  - Their minds are hostile to God, and cannot obey him (v 7).
  - They cannot please God (v 8). A mind acting out of hostility to God cannot do anything that is pleasing to him, even if the act itself is good.

- **"live in accordance with the Spirit"?**
  - They have their minds set on what the Spirit desires (v 5).
  - This means they enjoy "life and peace" (v 6).

8. What do verses 9-11 tell us about Christians?

- We are "controlled" by the Spirit (v 9)—our direction of thought and behavior is set by the Spirit's agenda, not by our own desires.
- We have the Spirit (v 9). If we belong to Christ, we must have the Spirit living in us.
- Our bodies are dead because of sin (v 10)—there is still sin living in us, and our bodies are decaying and will one day die.
- Our spirits are alive (v 10), because the Spirit has made us spiritually alive—right with God—through receiving Christ.
- Someday, even our bodies will be totally renewed and made eternally alive by the Spirit (v 11), just as Christ's was.

9. How do people "die", and what is the way to "live" (v 13)?

We "die" if we live according to the sinful nature (i.e. refuse to receive Christ and have our minds directed by the Spirit). We "live" (are empowered by the Spirit) by attacking and killing our sin. This process of "putting to death" our sin is what older theologians call "mortification".

- **What does this look like in reality?**
  It means a ruthless, full-hearted resistance to sinful practice. It means to declare war on attitudes and behaviors that are wrong. A Christian doesn't play games with sin. We don't say, "I can keep this under control." We get as far away from it as possible. It means seeing our relationship with our sin as a war, which needs to end with our sinful acts or attitudes being put to death.

10. **How can we make sure we have our "minds set on what the Spirit desires" (v 5)?**
    By deliberately drilling into our minds and hearts the truths of the gospel. In order to make our minds instinctively preoccupied with Christ (as the Spirit is) and how to obey him, we need to teach our minds. We need actively to set our minds to thinking about the gospel when we have a "spare moment" and when we are facing a difficult issue or decision. Ways to help ourselves do this:
    - Read and meditate on Scripture.
    - Memorize great truths from Scripture.
    - Learn to think to ourselves, "What difference does the gospel make?" before we make a decision.
    - Remind each other that we are to live according to the Spirit's direction, particularly when we are comforting or counseling a fellow believer.

Explore More

○ *Read Colossians 3:1-14. How do Paul's words here help us to know how to set our minds on spiritual things?*
Verses 1-4: We do so as we remember who we are: people who died with Christ, who belong in heaven more than we do in this sinful world, and who will one day live with him in glory. Negatively, we are not to spend time thinking about "earthly things". Notice that both our minds and hearts—our thoughts and our affections—are to be set on what Christ has done, is doing, and will do for us.

○ *How will doing so show itself in our thoughts and lives?*
We will mortify the things that our earthly/sinful desires demand—see the list in verses 5-9. We will pursue what makes us more and more like our Creator (v 10, 12)—see the list in verses 12-14.

11. **What motivations throughout the passage have there been to "put to death the misdeeds of the body" (v 13)?**
    - The Spirit lives in us to free us from the power of sin (v 2)—so we can kill it. We must never think a sin is too powerful for us to defeat.
    - Allowing sin to direct us leads to a present "death" (v 6)—killing it will bring us "life and peace."
    - We will one day enjoy sinless bodies (v 11)—and the Spirit enables us to start enjoying that now, more and more.
    - We have an obligation to Christ (v 12)—as we remember what Christ has done for us, we want to obey him out of gratitude.

- **How can we motivate ourselves to do this?**
- **How can we encourage each other to do this?**
    Sin can only be cut off at the root if we expose ourselves constantly to the unimaginable love of Christ for us. That exposure stimulates a wave

of gratitude. So we need to preach "grace mini-sermons" to ourselves during the day (and preach the same to others), particularly when we are tempted. For instance: "Jesus died for me, and he had to because of sins like this! Will I respond by sinning? Jesus died for me so I could enjoy the Spirit and the life of peace! Will I throw that away right now? I am in right relationship with God because he sent his Son to die for me and he sent his Spirit into me. Will I push him away by doing this?"

2

Glorious Adoption
Romans 8:14-39

The Big Idea
God has adopted Christians as his children, with wonderful privileges. He will bring them to his renewed creation and is working for their good in all things; so it is always worth keeping going in faith.

Summary
This section is all about divine adoption. If we want to understand who a Christian is, and why being a Christian is a privilege, we need to appreciate what it means that we are "sons of God" (v 14) and "God's children" (v 16).

Adoption was a much more customary legal procedure in Roman society than it was in Hebrew or Near Eastern culture. Paul, as a Roman citizen, would have been familiar with it. Adoption usually occurred when a wealthy adult had no heir for his estate. He would then adopt someone as heir—it could be a child, a youth, or an adult. The moment adoption occurred, several things were immediately true of the new son. First, his old debts and legal obligations were paid; second, he got a new name and was instantly heir of all the father had; third, his new father became instantly liable for all his actions (his debts, crimes, etc.); but fourth, the new son also had new obligations to honor and please his father. All this lies behind the passage here.

In this section, Paul lays out who is a son of God (those, both male and female, who have the Spirit through faith in Christ, v 14); what the privileges of sonship are (v 15-17; see question 3); why it is worth suffering as a child of God (v 18-25); how God helps us in the present (v 26-28); and how we can therefore be confident that nothing can happen that will stop our Father loving us (v 29-39).

Optional Extra

Ask your group to bring in pictures of their families (perhaps, unless you know it will stir up difficult memories, pictures of their parents or grandparents). Take in all the pictures, and then ask the group to match the group member to the picture, based on family resemblance. Lead into a discussion of what family characteristics group members have inherited. Return to this idea after question 3.

NOTE: If people in your group have been adopted, but have children of their own, it would be better to ask for photos of people's children, and have the same discussion about family resemblances.

Guidance for Questions

1. **If you could become a member of a famous family, which family would you choose, and why?**

   This is an introduction to the truth that when we put our faith in Christ, we are adopted into God's family (see questions 2-4). You group may choose to take this question seriously or humorously. Bear in mind that some members of your group may have difficult family backgrounds or have been adopted.

2. **How does Paul describe the identity of those who are "led by the Spirit"—i.e. people with faith in Christ?**

   They are "sons of God" (v 14).

   NOTE: In verses 14-27, Christians are three times called "sons" of God (v 14, 15, 19) and three times "children" (v 16, 17, 21). Some prefer gender-neutral language, but Paul is using "sons" because sonship was a status of privilege and power. (See comment on adoption on page 14.) So in using "sons" of Christians, Paul is saying that all believers, male and female, are now God's heirs. Christian women should not object to being called "sons" any more than Christian men should object when called Christ's "bride" (Ephesians 5:24-25; Revelation 19:7-8; 21:2).

3. **What are the privileges of being an adopted son of God?**

   Point out to your group that there is more than one privilege in Romans 8:15 and 17.

- **v 15**
  - *Security*—we don't need to fear, because we're sons. A good child-parent relationship is not characterized by fear that bad performance will end the relationship.
  - *Status*—as we move about in the world, we know our Father owns the place!
  - *Intimacy*—we call God "Abba." This is an Aramaic word best translated as "Daddy." Christians approach the all-powerful Creator as their dad.

- **v 16**

  Assurance—the Spirit of God gives us assurance ("testifies") that we truly are in God's family. This appears to be an inner witness in the heart—a sense that yes, God really does love me.

- v 17
  - *Inheritance*—"we are heirs." This means we have an incredible future. What is in store for us is so grand and glorious that it will be as though we each had alone gotten most of the glory of God. (We'll see more of this in verses 19-22.)
  - *Family resemblance*—"We share in his sufferings." When Jesus lived on earth, he suffered; his brothers and sisters will too, as they live and speak for him. When we suffer, we get to be like him! Paul sees this as a privilege.

4. **What difference does it make to us that we know God as a Father, not simply as a Master?**

   Every difference! We tend to functionally believe that God is our Master and so our relationship with him is based on our performance. We are always afraid of being "fired." The Spirit wipes all that away; we are children, not slaves, and so our relationship is based on unconditional love, not performance standards. Here are some contrasts (your group may not think of all of them, and may think of some additional ones, and that does not matter):

   A slave…
   - obeys because he or she has to.
   - fears punishment for breaching rules.
   - is always insecure.
   - focuses on keeping external rules.
   - works to keep this relationship.

   A child…
   - obeys out of love for their father.
   - recognizes any punishment as loving discipline.
   - is always secure.
   - focuses on relationships.
   - works because they have this relationship.

5. **How does Paul answer that question in verse 18? How are his words stronger than simply saying, "Yes, it is"?**

   He says that whatever we suffer now (remember, Paul suffered more than most of us ever will), it does not compare with what awaits us. This is the most emphatic "yes"—it is not that the future benefits just about outweigh all we go through now; it is that the worst of what anyone faces in this life is incomparable with all that a Christian will enjoy in the future.

6. **Why? What does Paul say is in store for…**

- **the creation?**

   It will be liberated from its bondage to decay. Currently, creation is frustrated (v 20), decaying (v 21), and in pain (v 22). It is not what it was created to be; creation involves pain, suffering and death. But not forever. One day, all that will be reversed; there will be fulfillment, newness, and joy. It will be liberated: free to be itself.

- **the children of God?**

   We will also enjoy "glorious freedom" (v 21). Verses 19 and 23 explain something of what this means. "The sons of God will be revealed" probably means that our sonship will be made publicly evident, and we'll be made completely like Christ (see verse 29). "The redemption of our bodies" (v 23) means we will have physical bodies, but without the limitations of sinful decay.

o **OPTIONAL: What view should Christians have of nature, based on these verses? What views will the Christian reject?**
Christians are to see the material world as inherently good, yet fallen. God's first commandment to the newly created Adam and Eve was to rule over and care for his creation (Genesis 1:28). This tells us two things: that God himself cares about the created world, and that we are supposed to care for it as well, as his stewards. Though the world now groans under the abuse and misuse it suffers, we are to care for it in every way possible. Equally, we should be committed to culture and creative pursuits.

We do not see the material world as inherently evil (many Christians have this view)—we're not to think that it's "spiritual" to avoid physical pleasures and/or to withdraw from the world, and denigrate art and culture-building. Equally, we're not to think of this material world as all there is, to live for physical pleasure and beauty, and/or virtually worship art and culture-building.

7. How should we be waiting for the day we see our Father face to face?
- **v 23**
"Eagerly." We are not to allow ourselves to be satisfied with the world and our lives as they are now. We're to look forward to our glorious future and not live as though this is all there is.

- **v 25**
"Patiently." We're to remember that we are not in glorious freedom yet; we shouldn't expect or demand everything to be perfect now, trying to drag perfection into our present. It isn't here yet; we must wait for God's timing.

8. When is it hardest to do these things (i.e. your answers to question 7)? What difference would being eager and/or patient make at those moments?
Since the world around us tends to live as though this is all there is, it is neither eager nor patient about the future. So there is always pressure to settle for what we have now—to see our work or family or hobby as the most important thing. Equally, there is always pressure to try to grab all we think we need right now—to change or leave a relationship, to trample on others to grasp a promotion, to be impatient and change our circumstances. Your group will hopefully be able to think of particular ways that these pressures come in their lives and your culture. Think through what being both eager and patient means.

9. **What is it (v 28)?**
   God's purpose in all circumstances is for the Christian's best. In every single aspect of our life, God is working for our good.

- **How does verse 29 help us understand what "the good" that God wants for his children is?**
   God has "predestined" that we will be "conformed to the likeness of his Son." So God works in everything that happens to us to change our character to be more and more like that of Jesus—he is working to make us as loving, noble, true, wise, strong, good, joyful and kind as Jesus is. This is crucial. "Our good" is to become more like Christ—verse 28 is not promising that God will give us an easier life, nor that what we think is "good" will be what he gives us.

Explore More

◦ *How do we see Paul living out what he says in Romans 8:28-29?*
◦ *2 Corinthians 12:7-9*
   Paul was given "a thorn in my flesh"—a persistently painful affliction of some sort. He asked God to change his circumstances (v 8)—but he accepted that God was working through his weakness, to demonstrate his glory and keep Paul humble, not conceited (v 7, 9). This was a very painful circumstance—but Paul knew that God was using it to work for his good and God's glory, and so he "boast[ed] ... gladly" about this weakness he had. His pain brought him closer to God, rather than hardening him against God.

◦ *Philippians 3:10-11*
   Paul's priority is not for an easy life but to "know Christ" and "become like him," even though this involves circumstances of suffering and death. His highest good is the good God is working in him—to make him more Christ-like.

NOTE: The Getting Personal section before question 10 (see page 17) mentions that God is working for our good in our failings. The point is that God's purposes for us cannot be ruined by our own sin. Sin is always bad, and we experience its painful consequences in our lives; but Romans 8:28-29 means that God is so great that he weaves it into our ultimate good. He can use even our failings to humble and teach and change us.

10. **What do each of the verbs in verses 29-30 mean, do you think?**
    Encourage your group to think hard about what they mean, rather than you simply reading out these definitions!
    - **Foreknew**: When God knows someone, it means he has set his love on them in a personal way (e.g. in Matthew 7:23, when Jesus says, "I never knew you," it doesn't mean he never knew about them but that he never had a relationship

with them). To be foreknown is to be loved by God back before the beginning of time.
- *Predestined*: To set a destination; to make a plan ahead of time. God, because he foreknew (foreloved) us, set our destination as being with him in glory, conformed to the image of Christ.
- NOTE: The word "predestined" often raises many questions. These will be dealt with more fully in the next study. For now, Paul is not wanting to raise a philosophical debate; rather, he wants to give us confidence about who we are and what God has done and will do for us.
- *Called*: The time or moment when God worked in us to awaken us to the truth of the gospel.
- *Justified*: Pronounced and treated by God as legally righteous and blameless because of the work of Christ in his life and death. This status is transferred to us when we believe in him. (The whole book of Romans is about this!)
- *Glorified*: To have all sin eradicated and be made perfect in body and soul.

○ **OPTIONAL: Why can Paul use the past tense "glorified" even though it has not yet happened, do you think?**
Because it is just as certain as any other part of God's purposes for his people.

- **How do they give us confidence?**
God finishes what he started! The key insight here is that each verb refers to the same set of people. Anyone who has been called—a Christian—has been foreknown and predestined and called and justified, and will be glorified.

11. **How do Paul's questions and answers in verses 31-39 help us when we...**
- **are afraid (v 31)?**
Whoever or whatever is opposed to us, God is for us. He is working for our good, he will glorify us, and nothing is out of his control. No need to fear!

- **are unsure that we will keep going as Christians (v 32)?**
God gave us his own Son to die for us so that we can live in glory with him. Since he gave us his precious Son, he will certainly give us everything else we need to keep going to glory.

- **feel guilty (v 33-34)?**
God has justified us, finding us not guilty because of Christ's death. It doesn't matter what anyone else says; we are righteous. The only condemnation we need fear is God's—and Christ, our risen Savior, is speaking on our behalf to him, so there can never be condemnation from God for us.

- **worry about whether God loves us (v 35-39)?**
Though we may suffer greatly (v 35-36), there is nothing in the future or in creation or in the spiritual realm that can change and separate us from

God's love. He loves us because he chose to love us (he foreknew us), not because of anything in us or anything around us. So whatever changes, his love will not.

12. How does this passage tell us...
(This question summarizes all the wonderful truths that this passage has taught.)
- **who we are?**
Refer back to questions 2-4.
- **whether living with Jesus as Lord is worth it?**
Refer back to questions 5-8.
- **whether we might get lost on the way to our home with our heavenly Father?**
Refer back to questions 9-11.
- OPTIONAL: *What difference should each of these make to our lives this coming week?*
- OPTIONAL: *Which truth has particularly thrilled you today?*

3

Sovereign Mercy

Romans 9:1 – 10:4

The Big Idea
God is the one who saves us, through electing us to have faith in the gospel. We are responsible for our rejection of the gospel.

Summary
This is not an easy passage! In dealing with the truth that the majority of the Jews—God's Old Testament people—have rejected Jesus as the Christ, and therefore that a growing majority of the church is Gentile, Paul deals with the issue of why people do not believe the gospel. His answer is that people do not believe because God has not chosen them to have faith; and yet people who do not believe are responsible for their refusal to trust Christ because they have hardened their hearts to the truth about God. We are therefore dealing with the issue of God's election—his sovereign decision to choose some sinful, undeserving people to receive his mercy by putting their faith in his Son—and with the doctrine of predestination.

Paul looks to the Old Testament to prove both that not everyone born in Abraham's family (the Jews) is a member of God's people and to show that membership of God's people has always been by God's merciful election. And at the end of the next study, we will see (in 11:33-36) Paul praising God for his wisdom, both in what he has revealed to us and what he has not. So, while there are many difficult issues involved in understanding Romans 9, and while the truths here are often difficult to accept, these verses should cause us to praise God. Question 9 aims to encourage your group to do this.

To prepare to teach through this study and the next one, you would find it helpful to read the relevant chapters (numbers 4 – 6) in *Romans 8–16 For You*, along with the appendix at the back entitled "The Doctrines of God's Sovereignty and Election." Don't let the study be sidetracked by these issues, however—offer to meet up outside the group time with members who have more questions, or ask (beforehand!) one of your pastors to set aside time to meet with anyone who would like to.

Optional Extra

Hand around some fairly good cookies to your group members. Then give a much nicer piece of cake to one group member, for no particular reason. Once other group members have noticed this, talk about the fairness of your action—whether you had the right to choose to be particularly kind to one member of your group; whether it would have been fairer to give no one that kindness; whether, having done it for one, you are bound to do it for everyone; and so on. You don't need to come to neat conclusions, but it leads into the whole area of how God is very kind to choose to elect some sinners to receive undeserved mercy, and not unjust in not choosing all sinners.

Guidance for Questions

1. **What does the idea of God's "election" mean to you? How do you feel when you think about it?**

   Your group may not know what "election" means, in which case go quickly to question 2. But your group may have some misunderstandings, or be very troubled about election, and this question will enable you to see this.

2. **How does Paul feel about the fact that most of his fellow Jews have rejected Jesus as their King and Savior?**

   "Great sorrow and unceasing anguish" (v 2). He wishes that he himself were cut off from Christ and eternal life with him, if that would somehow bring his Jewish cousins to faith in the Messiah. This is staggering! Here is a glimpse of Paul's love for his people.

3. **Paul says that God's word—his promise to save and bless Abraham's descendants—has not failed, even though most members of the nation of Israel have rejected Jesus as Lord (v 6). Why not (v 6, 8)?**
   - **v 6**

     "Not all who are descended from Israel are Israel." Some who are racially descended from Abraham, Isaac, and Jacob are not true Israel (i.e. not part of God's people).

- **v 8**

    God's children are those who are "children of the promise"—those whom God blesses—rather than "the natural children"—those who are born into Abraham's biological family tree.

- **Read Genesis 16:1-4a, 15-16; 17:15-22. How do we see the truth of Romans 9:6 in what happened to Abraham's children, Isaac and Ishmael?**

    Abraham (aka Abram) had two sons—Ishmael and Isaac. He had Ishmael by his wife, Sarah's, slave-girl, Hagar, because Sarah (aka Sarai) could not have children (16:1-4, 15-16). But God promised to give Sarah a child, impossible though that seemed (17:16)—and this son, Isaac, would be the one with whom God would "establish [his] covenant … as an everlasting covenant" (v 19). So we see that not all of Abraham's children were members of God's covenant people (i.e. the people he was committed to, and would bless with relationship with him): "Not all … Israel are Israel."

4. What did God tell Rebekah about her twins (v 12)?

    "The older [Esau] will serve the younger [Jacob]." Usually, the older son would inherit from the father, and the younger would be subservient to him—so in this case, it would have been expected that Esau would have inherited God's blessing. But God tells Rebekah that in fact the roles will be reversed—that the younger one will be the one who is part of God's covenant people, and not the older. For the whole story, see Genesis 25:21-34.

- **What reasons for God blessing Jacob and not Esau does Paul rule out (v 11, 12)?**
    - v 11: Anything good or bad in either of them. The choice was not based on what God knew about how the two boys would turn out.
    - v 12: The phrase "not by works" reinforces the point of verse 11. It is not that God simply foresaw who would accept and who would reject him. God's choice was nothing to do with anything in either Esau or Jacob.

- **Is any positive reason given for God's election of Jacob? What is it?**

    Yes. The only difference between the two was "God's purpose in election" (v 11). God chose to put Jacob above Esau simply because that was his purpose. The reason he told Rebekah that the younger would serve the older before they were born, Paul says, is so that it would be clear that the reason why Jacob inherited the blessing was God's election. Again, verse 12 reinforces this: the reason why Jacob was blessed was not because of him, but because of the choice of "him who calls."

    NOTE: Verse 13 sounds very harsh! But we must be careful not to think of this hatred as identical to the emotion we ordinarily call by that name. There is a Hebrew way of speaking behind this. It is a way of making a strong comparison, rather than saying that God really hated Esau. See Luke 14:26, where Jesus, who taught his followers to uphold the commandments (including to honor their parents) told them to "hate" their father and mother. That does not mean literally to hate them, but to prefer Jesus over them. Romans 9:13 is simply another way of saying that God chose that Jacob would inherit his promise, not Esau.

5. **On whom does God have mercy (v 15)?**
On anyone he chooses to.

- **What does salvation therefore not depend on (v 16)?**
"On man's desire or effort"—that is, on anything we want or strive for or achieve. Salvation is not our right. It can never be owed to us.

6. **How does this help us to think through whether God is being unjust to choose some and not others?**
Nobody has any claim upon God's mercy. (If they did, it would no longer be mercy.) "The wages of sin is death" (6:23), and we are all sinful. So no one can accuse God of unfairness in not extending his mercy to more people than he chooses to. Since God owes no one salvation, he is free to give it to (a) all, (b) some, or (c) none.

You could share this story with your group to illustrate the point. A rich person decided to choose twenty inner-city kids and guarantee their full college tuition. There were literally thousands of equally worthy recipients. And the rich man could have helped a lot more than twenty children. But could anyone say that since he helped some, he was being unfair to everyone else? No. He had no particular obligation to help any of the children. Since all he gave was sheer, free mercy, there could be no talk of him being unjust for not choosing a different twenty, or choosing twenty-two, and so on.

No one deserves to be saved. In one sense, justice demands that we all be condemned (and, without the cross, condemnation would be all we could receive from a just God). So the shock is not that God does not extend his compassion to everyone, but that he extends it to anyone.

NOTE: This is not an easy question or issue. You might want to read out the above answer to your group and then let them respond to the teaching.

7. **Read Exodus 4:21; 7:3; 10:1. Who hardened Pharaoh's heart?**
God.

- **Read Exodus 8:15, 19; 9:7, 17, 27. Who hardened Pharaoh's heart?**
Pharaoh.

8. **What are we reminded of in Romans 9:19-21 about…**
- **God?**
He made us ("formed" us); therefore he has rights of ownership over us.

He has the right to do what he wants in and with his world.

- **ourselves?**

  We have no right to "talk back to God" (v 20). We are so far below God—the distance between the potter and the clay—that we have neither the wisdom nor the authority to question our Creator. We must beware of standing in judgment over God.

9. **How does the teaching of verses 1-29...**

- **help us to worship God?**

  If we understand who God is—our sovereign Creator, who is in control of everything—and what God has done for us as Christians—chosen us, sent his Son to die for us, and given us mercy—we will be deeply thankful to God for doing everything.

- **humble us?**

  Since God's people are only saved because of God's choice and his mercy, we will be joyful but also very realistic and humble about ourselves. Nothing we are, and nothing we have done or can ever do, will earn our salvation. We did not even choose to trust God—he chose to be merciful to us!

- **make us hopeful for non-Christians?**

  God can save anyone. There was a time when we did not know God, and left to ourselves we would have continued to have hard hearts. Then God broke in, softened our hearts, and saved us. Since he did that for us, he can do that for anyone. God's election emboldens our evangelism.

- **give us confidence that we will reach heaven?**

  God has chosen us to be part of his people, eternally. He is the one who gets each of us to heaven—it is not up to us. See Romans 8:28-39.

10. **Israel did not attain righteousness—they had not ended up being in right relationship with God. Why not (9:30 – 10:3)?**

    - Because they pursued righteousness "by works" (9:32). Because they sought to create their own righteousness as a way to stand before God, they stumbled over the concept that God's righteousness must come as a gift from him (end of verses 32-33). The Jews wanted to be right with God (they "pursued" it, v 31) but tried to find it in the wrong way. Paul makes the same point in 10:3.

    - Though they were zealous, they did not base their zeal on knowledge. They were willing to go to great lengths to obey God; they were very sincere in their beliefs; but their beliefs were mistaken. They refused to accept that God was offering his righteousness through faith in Christ. Notice that Paul is overturning a common proverb of our time: "It doesn't matter what you believe as long as you are sincere." In truth, zeal without knowledge is fanaticism; it refuses to reflect on its own incorrectness.

- **What does verse 4 say is the way in which God has made it possible to be right with him?**
  Christ. "Everyone who believes" in him is right with God.

○ *OPTIONAL: What do you think Paul means in verse 4 when he says, "Christ is the end of the law"?*
  If your group is struggling, ask the following question to help them:

○ *OPTIONAL: When someone becomes a Christian, what do they now know the law cannot do for them, which Christ has done for them?*
  Christians know that obeying the law cannot save them, but that they do not need to seek salvation that way, because Christ has saved them through his law-keeping life and sin-bearing death. Christ's work shows that the law as a way to seek righteousness is ended, so that faith may be seen as the way of righteousness. The Christian no longer sees the law as a system of salvation, though we are still obligated to obey the law as a way to please the God who has saved us by grace and express our gratitude to him.

11. **Who is responsible for someone being saved?**
    (This is an opportunity to sum up the main thrust of the teaching in Romans 9.) God. We can only be saved if God graciously elects to have mercy on us by giving us saving faith in his Son.

- **Who is responsible for someone not being saved?**
  That person is, just as Pharaoh was. God gives us over to our stubborn rejection of him. We decide to resist God; God gives us what we choose, and reinforces us in that position. Yes, God hardens our hearts, but he does so simply by passing over someone and letting them have the way they have chosen.

12. **How would you use Romans 9 to explain to a Christian friend (in as simple a way as you can!)…**
    - **what we mean by God's election?**
      This will help your group to explain the content of this passage in a summarized, clear way. You could split into pairs and each take turns to explain Paul's teaching here.

    - **why it is good news for them?**
      As we will see in the next study, Paul's consideration of God's sovereign purposes and merciful election causes him to break into spontaneous worship (11:33-36). God's election is something we may need to wrestle with, but it is good news. Without it, no one would be saved. And without it, no Christian could be confident that they would reach eternal life. It is very good news that God graciously has mercy on those he chooses, and commits to bring them home to heaven.

○ *OPTIONAL: What questions or issues surrounding the doctrines of election and predestination do you need to think more about, or research?*

Your group may well have questions and tensions surrounding this doctrine, both intellectual and emotional—and it is good to air those, wrestle with them, and pray to God about them. Encourage your group members, if they are feeling unsettled by the content of this study, to keep thinking the issues through.

Some useful resources to point people to: Romans 8–16 For You, where I deal with this chapter in more depth, and you will also find an appendix looking at the doctrine of God's sovereign election. J.I. Packer's Evangelism and the Sovereignty of God is also very useful, as are the following chapters in Dr. Packer's Concise Theology: Sovereignty; Definite Atonement; Election; Predestination; Inability; Illumination; Effectual Calling; Justification.

4

The Gospel and Israel
Romans 10:5 - 11:36

The Big Idea
God has planned to save Jews and non-Jews, and is powerful to do so; the right response to his sovereign plan of election is not to try to understand it completely but to praise his wisdom and power.

Summary
This is another difficult passage of Scripture. Chapter 10 establishes once more how someone can be saved—and Paul uses Moses to teach his point, to make clear that this has always been the way of salvation: i.e. it is not by what we do, but what we believe (v 5-13). This truth should lead believers to communicate this message (v 13-17).

Paul then moves on to clarify the truth that Israel has no excuse for rejecting God. They have heard and understood the message that salvation is by grace, not by works (v 18-21); they have not believed because they are disobedient and obstinate (v 21). This is an amazing indictment. God has "held out [his] hands" to the Jews in a way he has not to the Gentiles; yet the Gentiles have responded better than the Jews.

Therefore the question remains: has God rejected Israel (11:1)? Paul immediately answers with a big "No!" The rest of the chapter details why, and Paul's central argument is that God has not rejected Israel because Israel's unbelief is not total:

- Paul is a Jewish believer (v 1).
- There have been times before when it looked as though Israel had rejected God and he them, as in Elijah's time—but God had in fact reserved a faithful remnant (v 2-4).
- In the present, there are Jewish Christians, chosen by grace (v 5-6).
- In the future, many Jews will turn to Jesus as the Christ and be saved (v 11-15, 25-32).

The application for non-Jewish Christians is therefore not to be arrogant or complacent (v 20-22); to be hopeful about the Jews, even though the Jews oppose them (v 23-24); and to worship and praise God for his wisdom and plan, even when (or especially when) we do not understand it (v 33-36).

Optional Extra

Share some testimonies of Jews who have become Christians. You will find some at: www.cwi.org.uk/judaism/testimonies.html or in the book *The Unusual Suspects* (Christian Focus). This would best be done after question 1 or question 6.

NOTE: Pointing to these testimonies of Jews coming to faith in Christ does not mean that either the author or publisher of this Good Book Guide agree with or espouse every opinion given by those recounting their testimonies.

Guidance for Questions

1. **Are there people or groups of people who, deep down, you think will never become Christians? Why do you think that?**

In Paul's day, it would have appeared to many that the Jews would never come to faith in Christ—that their rejection was total, and final. Paul is going to say that it is not—that many will be saved. In our day, there will be individuals or peoples who, if we are honest, we think will never trust Christ: perhaps because they have strong beliefs in a different religion, or have rejected the gospel repeatedly, or have grown up in a very secular, materialistic home, and so on. Thinking like this will show itself in how we pray (or don't pray) for them, and how we speak to them.

You could come back to the people/peoples your group mentions here when you reach the Getting Personal after question 6.

2. **How does Moses say someone can be saved, in verse 5?**

By doing (i.e. obeying) the law—Moses seems to be teaching the possibility of getting salvation ("life") through law-keeping.

- **What is the problem with seeking to be saved in this way?**

No one can keep the law perfectly! See Romans 2:1-6; 3:9-20. Because we are sinful, the law is not a way for us to achieve eternal life; instead, it shows us that we are not righteous, and that we need saving (v 20). So in Romans 10:5, Moses' quote is simply saying, *If you could obey the law perfectly, you would receive eternal life.* But we can't do that.

- **What does he say about a different way to be saved in verse 8?**
  There is a word (something to say or believe) that is "near you." In other words, God has brought salvation to us, and we need only believe "in your mouth and in your heart." Salvation, Moses says, is to do with believing something in your heart and therefore saying it with your mouth. It is a "word of faith" (v 8).

  ○ **OPTIONAL: If your group are struggling, explain that "the word" is something that saves us. Then ask, Where is the word that saves, when it is saving someone?**
  In their mouth and in their heart. So this is about something to be believed and stated, not something to be done or achieved.

- **What does Paul say more specifically about this different way, now that Jesus has lived, died, and risen (v 9-13)?**
  Paul tells us what this saving "word" to believe and speak of is. It means there is now…
  - *a truth to be known*: about Jesus' identity—he is "Lord"; and about his work—he was raised from the dead (and thus he must have died). So we must know that Jesus is God ("Lord" is a way of referring back to Yahweh, God's Old Testament name) and that he died for our sins and rose to give new life.
  - *a truth to be believed*: we must believe this truth in our hearts, trusting our whole self to the person and work of Christ as our righteousness.
  - *a truth to be stated*: to confess with the mouth is simply part of believing with the heart. If we truly believe internally, we will be loyal in what we say.
  - *a truth that, when believed, saves (v 11)*: we will never regret trusting in Christ instead of ourselves.
  - *a salvation that is for anyone (v 12-13)*: There is no difference between Jew and Gentiles when it comes to the need for Christ's salvation, nor when it comes to its availability.

3. **What should the truths of verses 9-13 lead believers to do (v 14-15)? Why?**
   How do people come to call on Christ's name and be saved? By believing (v 14); so they need to hear about him (v 14); and for this to happen, the message must be communicated or "preached" (v 14); and so someone must be "sent" to do the communicating (v 15). Paul has in mind not just the sending of the apostles, but the sending of ordinary Christians. God has sent us with the "beautiful" message of salvation. We know that everyone needs to call on Christ to be saved, and that anyone can do this, and so we will

seek to bring them this beautiful good news.

Explore More

- *In verses 16-21, Paul returns to his original question: why haven't the Jews believed? What possibilities does he raise, and how does he answer them?*
  - *v 18*
    Perhaps they have not heard. Of course they have. Paul quotes from Psalm 19, which is a little surprising because it speaks of how God's creation declares his glory (not how his people declare the gospel). Paul probably means that the spread of the gospel was as widespread as that. (Remember, Paul is thinking of the Jews here, not the entire population of the 1st-century world. Wherever a Jewish community existed, the gospel had been preached.) They had heard.
  - *v 19-20*
    Perhaps Israel did not understand. But, Paul says in verse 19, in the Old Testament it was the Gentiles who did not understand, and yet God had overcome their lack of understanding (v 20). Israel had far more understanding than the Gentiles did of God's nature, the need to be right with him, the promises of forgiveness by substitution implicit in the tabernacle and temple worship, the promises of a Messiah, and the fact that God would become our righteousness for us (see Jeremiah 23:5-6). They understood enough.
  - ***What is the right answer, in verse 21?***
    They were disobedient and obstinate. This is an amazing indictment. God had held out his hands to Israel, but though they had heard and understood, they refused God's invitation to faith and insisted they would earn their own righteousness.

---

4. **What evidence is there that God hasn't rejected them:**
- **in the present (v 1)?**
  Paul himself! Paul is saying, *Look at me. I am a Jew and was very hardened to the gospel. How can we say that God has given up on the Jews when he didn't give up on me?*
- **from the past history of Israel (v 2-6)?**
  800 years before, God's prophet Elijah lived in a time when Israel persecuted believers, and he thought he was "the only one left" (see 1 Kings 19:14). But God contradicted Elijah's perception—God had not given up on Israel, but rather had "reserved for myself seven thousand who have not bowed the knee to Baal" (a false, rival god).

  In other words, there had always been a faithful remnant in Israel—the spiritual Israel within Israel—even during times when it seemed that Israel had utterly rejected God, and he them. Paul says in Romans 11:5-6 that this is still the case at "the present time."

5. What has happened because of Israel's "transgression" (that is, their rejection of the gospel) (v 11-12)?

It has brought salvation to the Gentiles. Because there was a lot of hostility to Christianity among the majority of the Israelites, the early Jewish Christians were unable to conclude that the gospel was only for ethnic Israel; and they went and preached the gospel to Gentiles, bringing the "riches" of the gospel to "the world."

- **What effect does Gentile conversion have on Israel, and how does this affect Paul's ministry (v 11, 13-14)?**

  It makes Israel "envious." (This is not the sinful envy of covetousness, where you want what your neighbor has or want them not to have it because you don't. Here, what is being envied—salvation—is something God desires all his people to enjoy.) So one of Paul's goals in his ministry of evangelizing the Gentiles is to "arouse my own people to envy and save some of them" (v 14). The Jews will see many Old Testament promises fulfilled in the Gentile Christians, and believe.

  NOTE: A possible example of this is in Acts 6:1-7. The early church set aside deacons to care for the needy, and a lot of Jewish priests then converted to Christ. Why? The priests were supposed to bring the people's contributions to the poor, but that did not happen very well. Now the Christians, under the power of the Holy Spirit, were generous and creating a community in which every needy person was cared for. That was what Israel was supposed to be (Deuteronomy 15:4-5)—but wasn't. It seems the priests saw it and were "envious," and listened to the gospel and came to faith.

6. If your church is largely non-Jewish, are you a community that is living out the fulfillment of what God called Old Testament Israel to be? How? And how could you do this more?

- **Would a devout Jew look at your church and be aroused to envy, so that they give the gospel a hearing?**

  You might like to think about these Old Testament passages, and how well your church reflects the priorities God sets for his people: Exodus 23:9 ("foreigner" = not a member of ancient Israel); Deuteronomy 15:4-5; Jeremiah 22:3; Micah 6:8.

7. What is Paul wanting the Gentile Christians to do or not do?

- **v 18-21**

  Not boast—they must not look down on the branches that have been broken off, i.e. the unbelieving Jews. Gentile Christians have been brought into the history and promises that come through Israel—we have a Jewish Bible and a Jewish Messiah. Further, Gentile Christians should not be arrogant, but rather reverently afraid (v 21). Since God did not spare Jews who did not trust Christ, he will not spare us if we cease to trust him.

- **v 22**

   Meditate on both the kindness and sternness of God. God is both kind (merciful) and stern (he judges)—and whether his kindness or sternness rests on you depends entirely on whether you believe or disbelieve. The example of disbelieving Israel should prevent any casual complacency, and encourage a resolve to "continue."

   NOTE: We should not pit this against 8:30 ("Those he justified, he also glorified") and other passages where Paul insists we are safe in Christ's love. This is not about losing a salvation you have; it is about the revelation of counterfeits. Jewish rejection of Christ showed that they were not truly members of God's people. If we have faith in Christ Jesus, we can be assured; but we must never be arrogant.

- **v 23 24   what should they believe?**

   That God can save the Jews. If he was able to save Gentiles ("wild [branches] by nature"), then "how much more" is he able to bring the Jews, the "natural branches," back "into their own olive tree!"

- *OPTIONAL: What would go wrong in your Christian life if you remembered only either the "kindness" or the "sternness" of God?*

   - *Only kindness—we will become complacent, assuming that we are saved. We will fall into the error of thinking that everyone is saved, or that "good people" are saved. We will assume we are saved, rather than relying on Christ.*
   - *Only sternness—we will become anxious, terrified of losing our salvation, and crushed by our own failure to live in a holy way. We will forget that we are saved by Christ, not by our performance.*

8. How does Paul say God views Israel (v 28)?

As beloved enemies. They have rejected the gospel and persecuted believers (see 1 Thessalonians 2:14-16), and so have made themselves God's "enemies on your account." Yet they are also loved, "on account of the patriarchs"—the Jews' ancestors to whom God made his promises to bless and save. So just as God loved every Christian when they were still an enemy (Romans 5:8), he loves Jewish non-Christians, though they are also his enemies.

9. How should this shape our view of Jewish non-Christians?

It is worth pointing your group to 11:30-31 here. We should see them with hope. God has reached us with his mercy through their disobedience; he is able to reach them through our faith. Just as God views Jews as his beloved enemies, so should his people—they are rejecting the gospel, but we should still love them and seek to bring the gospel to them and show them in our churches the fulfillment of God's promises to bless.

- **What practical difference should it make to you as a church and as individuals?**

  This will depend on where you live—whether there is any, or a sizeable, Jewish population nearby. At the least, it means praying for the Jews. It will likely mean more than this—practical outreach and seeking to come alongside Jews, in order to communicate the gospel to them.

10. **What is Paul praising God for here?**
    - The greatness of his wisdom and knowledge (v 33).
    - The fact that his judgments and plans are beyond our comprehension (v 34).
    - The truth that he does not owe us anything, and needs nothing from us (v 35).
    - The fact that everything comes from him, and exists for him (v 36).

11. **Why is it significant that this outbreak of spontaneous worship comes at the end of chapters 9 – 11?**

    Because Paul has been considering God's sovereign plans and his election of his people to salvation. These are things that cannot be fully understood (even by Paul!) and which cause lots of questions and tensions. Yet nevertheless, they lead Paul to praise God. Paul's study of truth moves him to worship. And he does not even get troubled by the aspects of God's ways which he cannot discern or figure out—instead, he praises God for them (11:33).

12. **Reread 9:1-5. Putting these verses alongside 11:33-36, what effect does Paul's knowledge of God's sovereign election of his people have on him?**

    It leads him to praise God and long to bring him glory (v 33-36); but it does not lessen his concern for those he knows who are not saved, nor his heartbreak that they will not trust Christ. Paul both praises God for his merciful election and weeps for those who have not (yet) been called by God to have faith in Christ.

- **How can this shape our own reaction to the truths of Romans 9 – 11?**

  We should mirror Paul. God's election should not make us feel cold toward those who are not saved, nor hopeless that they will not be saved. Rather, it fuels our confidence that they can be saved, so we will witness to them. At the same time, we should be very grateful to God for electing anyone at all, and so deeply humbled that he has had mercy on us. And we should praise him for being a God who is beyond us, who is merciful and just and sovereign.

5

New Relationships

Romans 12 – 13

The Big Idea

Because of what God has done for us, we live sacrificially for him, seeking to please him in all we do: in how we view ourselves, how we serve and love our church, and how we live in our nation and society.

Summary

Chapter 12 marks a turning point, the beginning of a new section. "Therefore" (v 1) shows that Paul is about to give an outline of Christian living that should issue from a knowledge of and trust in the gospel that he has been explaining. So 12:1-2 is a summary of the whole of the Christian life:

- *In view of God's mercy:* our lives should be lived in gratitude for what he's done for us.
- *Offer your bodies as living sacrifices:* our thanks shows itself in wholehearted, costly obedience to God, and this includes our bodies as well as our minds.
- *Holy and pleasing to God:* the gospel both frees us and motivates us to live lives that please our Creator. In Christ, we are able to please him.
- *This is your spiritual act of worship:* "spiritual" is better translated "logical." In other words, if you are thinking clearly about God's mercy, this way of living is the only rational response.
- *Do not be conformed, but be transformed:* we need to learn to reject the pattern of the world around us, and embrace God's will for our character and our life.

The rest of chapters 12 – 13 shows us how to be "living sacrifices" in these areas of our lives:

- how we view ourselves and our abilities (12:3-8).
- in the church, and toward those who persecute the church (v 9-21).
- as citizens of a state (13:1-7).
- toward our neighbor (v 8-10).
- in our perspective on the present and future (v 11-14).

Optional Extra

The passage finishes with Paul encouraging Christians to "clothe yourselves with the Lord Jesus Christ" (13:14). Our clothes show something of who we are; and they affect how we behave (see question 10). So show the group some pictures of people in their national dress, from around the world, and challenge them to guess which country they are each from. Discuss how wearing the national dress might make someone feel and/or behave differently.

Guidance for Questions

1. **If you had to sum up the Christian's approach to life in a sentence, what would you say?**

   This question is asking: *what difference does being a Christian, justified by faith, make to my day-to-day life, decisions, priorities, reactions, etc.?* There are no wrong answers—Paul is going to give us his summary of the whole Christian life in the first two verses of chapter 12.

2. **What does Paul "urge [his] brothers"—fellow Christians—to do? What does each mean?**

   - v 1

   "Offer your bodies as living sacrifices." This refers back to the burnt offerings sacrificed at the temple in the Old Testament. You might want to explain to the group what this was: you selected a valuable, blemish-free animal from your flock and offered it to God. This showed that all you had was at God's disposal—you were not giving God the leftovers!

   So to be a "living sacrifice" is to be fully at God's disposal, even when that means a cost to us. And it involves our "bodies." The right response to God is not simply inward and abstract; it is practical. Notice also that the word "living" means that the sacrifice is a constant thing. The Christian life is a daily giving over of our lives and our bodies in obedience to God. It is to die to ourselves, our desires and preferences, daily. (See Jesus' words in Luke 9:23-24.)

   - v 2

   "Be transformed by the renewing of your mind." We are to have our minds so fired by the gospel that we embrace God's way of thinking, feeling, and behaving—to know and love his will for our lives. This will mean that we no longer conform to how the world thinks and works—we will recognize and reject it.

3. **What motivation does Paul give in these verses for the hard work of Christian living?**

   - "Therefore, in view of God's mercy" (v 1). We give ourselves to God because of all that Paul has been explaining in Romans 1 – 11: namely, that we are justified by grace alone through faith alone because of Christ alone. We are motivated by gratitude for grace.

   - "Pleasing to God" (v 1). The gospel radically reorients our aim in life, so that we are no longer hoping and seeking to please ourselves, or even others, but our Father. (See 1 Thessalonians 2:4.) In Christ, God loves us and approves of us as his children—so now we are able to, and want to, please our Father.

   - "Your spiritual act of worship" (v 1). The word "spiritual" is literally "rational." The only logical response to mercy is to make a sacrificial offering of our lives. And this is how we worship God.

   - As we live this way and think this way, we will be "able to test and approve what God's will is" (v 2).

We will be able to understand God better, and how we can live a life that is "good."

○ **OPTIONAL: What other motivations might Christians have for living God's way? Why are they ineffective?**

The main alternative motivation is fear (although we can also live God's way in order to impress others, or feel successful). If fear is the primary motivation for our obedience, we will likely see the following effects:

- *Our motivation will lose its power over time. Fear moves you to great feats, but it is exhausting. Fear-based religion tends to be short-lived.*

- *We will have trouble with repenting. We think there is a line that if we cross it, if we sin too much, God will condemn us. So repentance is something we avoid, or do so with trembling, because we fear reprisals from God.*

- *We will see suffering as punishment. Trials make us think, "God is paying me back! God has abandoned me!" Or "This isn't fair—I obeyed God so that this kind of thing wouldn't happen, but it has!" Despair or bitterness will be the result of suffering if one's Christian life is fear-based.*

4. **How do we worship Christ? Why is this both exciting and challenging?**

By offering ourselves, every day, sacrificially to God. Worship is not less than Sunday gathered worship; but it is much more than that. It is a daily way of life. Worship is giving all of ourselves to Christ, who gave us all of himself. This is exciting because it means that we can, in every moment, worship the God who saved us. We can always be offering ourselves to him in worship out of gratitude. And so it is challenging, too, because Romans 12:1-2 indicates that our worship cannot be restricted to Sundays or to church events or to singing, and so on. These are all ways to worship; but worship is far more radical than that.

5. **How does this help us understand what it means to think of ourselves "with sober judgment" (v 3)?**

To think of ourselves with sober judgment means to see ourselves in terms of our gospel faith. Paul is saying, *All of you have been given your saving faith in Christ crucified, and that is how you are to measure yourself.* So we will not think of ourselves more highly than we ought—we are sinners; our efforts earn only judgment; we needed saving by Another. But equally, the gospel prevents us thinking in a more lowly way than we ought—we are *saved* sinners, loved and valued in the gaze of the only one whose opinion ultimately matters.

Sober judgment means evaluating ourselves in light of the gospel we believe.

6. **How else should we view ourselves (v 5-6a)?**

As one body (the church), having different gifts and who belong to each other. We are all different, and have been given distinct personalities, temperaments, histories, and abilities. This image of the body prevents us thinking more highly of ourselves than we ought (we need each other) and in too lowly a way (others need us). See 1 Corinthians 12:17-21.

- **What should we do with what God has given us (v 6b-8)?**

    Use his gifts for ministry—i.e. particular channels of service that focus on people's needs. Whatever God has enabled us to do, Paul says, "Let him use it … let him do it."

    NOTE: This is not an exhaustive list of gifts that God gives. Paul lists others in 1 Corinthians 12:8-10, 28 and Ephesians 4:11. In Romans 12, Paul mentions "prophecy." This is probably not the gift of giving divinely inspired messages from God. "In proportion to his faith" is saying that the prophet must not prophesy in a way that contradicts Christian doctrine—if prophecy were a divine word direct from God, why would such a rule be laid down? So here in Romans 12:6, it seems to mean preaching in its various forms.

7. **How do these verses show us what it means to be a "living sacrifice" in our relationships…**

- **within the church (v 9-16)?**

    "Love must be sincere" (v 9). Real love is very sacrificial, as Paul shows in the rest of this section. Ask your group to think about what each command means, what it looks like in reality, and how it involves being a living sacrifice. Here are some ideas:

    - Real love involves hating what is disobedient to God (v 9), even in those we love. A love that is afraid to confront someone we love where they are wrong is not really love, but a selfish desire to be loved by them. True love is willing to confront, even to risk the relationship, in order to help the person.
    - Real love is doggedly committed—it is devoted and brotherly (v 10a). There is a tie between Christians, just as in families, that cannot be broken.
    - Real love is putting others first—"honor one another above yourselves" (v 10). This is not to convince yourself you are inferior; it is to concentrate more on the needs of others than on your own. Verse 16 repeats this idea.
    - Real love is patient—this is what verses 11-12 are calling for.
    - Real love combines feeling with action. We are to empathize with others (v 15); but we are also to put our money where our mouth is (v 13).

    Here, we see that love is doing whatever it takes to give people whatever they need. It means you make sacrifices of emotion, action, and your rights.

- **toward those who persecute the church (v 17-21)?**

    The basic principle here is summarized at the beginning and end:

"Do not repay anyone evil for evil" (v 17); "Do not be overcome by evil, but overcome evil with good" (v 21). We are to live at peace with, rather than avoid, the hostile person (v 18); forgive and forgo any repayment or resentment (v 19); and express loving words and action toward them (v 20).

NOTE: There are boundaries to this. Verse 9 reminds us that we are not loving truly when we enable someone to sin. An enemy may be so aggressive that to have anything to do with them is to invite them to sin; so the "good" you can do is to stay away. We need to discern our own motives—are we seeking to bless or to pay back?

8. **What do these verses show us about how we can please God in our relationships with our state?**
   - Submit to its authority (v 1).
   - Submit according to conscience (v 5b). We do not obey simply so that we will not be punished, but because we know this is a way to obey God.
   - Submit respectfully (v 7). We are to comply with the authorities in a way that shows them respect, honor, and courtesy. Even if individuals in such positions of authority are not worthy of much respect, we show respect to the authority structure that stands under and behind them.

○ *OPTIONAL: What three reasons do these verses give for submitting?*
   - *It is right (v 1)—God has established these authorities.*
   - *It is wise (v 3-4)—governments are needed to hold people accountable in a way that makes it possible to live together. Without a state to "bear the sword," there would be chaos. We cannot all bear the sword—equally, we need someone to.*
   - *It is fair (v 6-7)—these verses suggest we submit because it is fair. Paul seems to be indicating that governing is hard work—we owe authorities respect and submission in return for the hard work of governing that they do.*

NOTE: You might like to remind your group that the authorities Paul was speaking of were at best unfriendly and at worst actively hostile toward the church. We cannot excuse non-submission on the grounds of our government not being Christian or pursuing Christian priorities.

Explore More

○ *In Romans 13:7, Paul is echoing Jesus' words [in Matthew 22:21]. What is Jesus saying about what we should give to "Caesar" (the state), and what we should not?*
We owe the state our taxes, but not our primary loyalty, or our worship. Some things belong to the state—everything belongs to God.

○ ***Read Exodus 1:17; Daniel 3:4-6; 6:7; Acts 5:29. What do these Bible passages show us about the limits of the Christian's duty to submit to the state?***

We do not have a duty to obey if…
- *(Exodus 1:17) the authorities command us to do something that would break God's moral laws—here, to kill the infant Israelite boys.*
- *(Daniel 3:4-6) the authorities command us to worship something other than God—here, worshiping the king as a deity.*
- *(Acts 5:29) the authorities command us not to do something that God has commanded—here, not speaking to others about Christ.*

---

9. What do verses 8-10 tell us about how we can truly love those around us?

We have a continuing debt to love each other, which is how we keep God's law. Yet the law itself is "summed up in this one rule: 'Love your neighbor as yourself'" (v 9). So God's law shows us how to love each other. The obedient thing is the loving thing. If we want to love others, we will obey God's law.

- **Why will this sometimes be unpopular with those we are trying to love?**

Because, in the short run (which is all that, humanly, we are able to see), it often seems loving to break God's law. For example, often we know that the truth will hurt someone, so we lie. Paul says we are not wiser than God in determining what is best for someone. But if we do not have this perspective, then we will often confuse "the loving thing" with "the comfortable thing" or "the popular thing."

10. What perspective should Christians have, and what difference will that perspective make (v 11-14)?

Each day of our lives, our salvation on the day when Jesus returns draws closer (v 11). The night (this world as it is now) will not go on much longer; the day (the eternal world) will break in any time now (v 12).

So we should put on "the armor of *light*" (v 12)—behave "as in the daytime" (v 13). We are to imagine that the day has dawned and that Jesus is right before us, and then ask, "Now, how would I behave? What is really eternally important? What will last forever?"

So we live as though we are "clothed" in Jesus (v 14). How you dress has an effect on your behavior. (If you wear a tuxedo or a long gown, you will behave differently than if you are wearing jogging clothes.) We need to remember what (or who) we are wearing—and behave accordingly.

11. How, specifically, can you as individuals live more sacrificially this week…
- **toward other members of your church?**
- **toward members of your community?**

- **in your relationships with your state/government?**

Each individual's circumstances are different, and what is sacrificial for one may not be so much for another (or may be impossible for another). So this question is not intended to provoke a competition between group members, nor to be a time for thinking of what other church members ought to be doing! You might choose to ask group members to write down their answers before sharing, or simply to write down without sharing.

Galatians 6:2-5 reminds us that while we are to share each other's burdens, we each carry our own load—our own set of circumstances and responsibilities; and these will affect greatly what it looks like for each of us to live sacrificially. E.g. one person may announce that they need to give $100 a month to your church. That may be very sacrificial for them; not sacrificial at all for another group member; and utterly impossible for a third.

12. **How can we encourage each other to live this way, even (or especially) when it is hard?**

This question encourages the group to finish where you started—with Romans 12:1. We must do all this "in view of God's mercy." Any other motivation will lead to being proud or being crushed. So we need to encourage one another by pointing each other to God's mercy to us, both in our day-to-day lives and supremely at the cross.

6

The Weak and the Strong

Romans 14:1 – 15:1

The Big Idea

All Christians have been saved in Christ, and belong to him. So we should not judge other Christians who do what we do not; and we should restrict our freedoms to serve those who do not do what we know to be allowed.

Summary

In this section, Paul applies all he has been saying about the gospel—how it saves and changes us—to a very specific case—a particular problem within the Roman congregation: the fact that Christians are "passing judgment" on fellow Christians when it comes to "disputable matters" (Romans 14:1). These matters seem to have included eating meat and foods the Old Testament identified as unclean; drinking alcohol; and observing particular holy days.

Paul challenges the weaker believers not to condemn those who disagree with them, to check their own position, and to remember that Christ has died and is the judge of all Christians. But, despite being a strong believer himself, he challenges the strong as well—they should not unthinkingly use their freedom (to eat meat, for instance), if, by doing so, they will encourage a weaker believer to sin by joining in with a behavior that they believe in conscience to be wrong.

The disputable matters in your church will likely be different; but the principles of 14:1-2, and the motivations and reasons Paul then gives through to 15:1, still apply in those areas.

Optional Extra

Give two members of your group a disputable statement. E.g. "Australia is the most beautiful country on earth"; "The Knicks will win the NBA next year"; "The 90s were the best decade to be a teenager." Ask one to defend the statement and the other to disagree with it, for a minute each, and then to reply to one another's points.

Then ask the rest of the group to weigh in with their opinions on each side. Let the discussion continue for a while, and then ask, "How did the disagreement cause you to feel? How did it change the way you felt about the members of the group who were disagreeing?"

The idea is to see that disagreements, even over matters that are not world-changing or life-threatening, cause us to see people differently, and eventually to treat them differently.

Guidance for Questions

1. **What causes avoidable disagreement and division in churches?**

   There are some disagreements and

divisions which, though tragic, are justified, due to false teaching. But many are avoidable—they are over what Paul calls "disputable matters" (14:1). This question does not ask your group to identify the subject of the disagreements but to think about the attitudes that lie behind them. The rest of the study will lay out Paul's teaching: that conflicts are often are caused by Christians condemning other believers for behavior which Scripture does not in fact forbid, or by Christians encouraging other believers to do what they in conscience think to be wrong through behaving in ways that are correct but the subject of the disagreement. You could refer back to your discussion after question 6 and/or question 9.

2. **What are the differences of opinion between them?**

- **v 2-3**

    Eating. Some felt that, as Christians, they could not eat meat.

- **v 5**

    Some felt they had to observe certain days as holy (perhaps Jewish / Old Testament feast days—see Colossians 2:16).

- **v 14, 20**

    "Unclean" foods. This is a reference to Old Testament ceremonial laws about foods that were clean and unclean (e.g. Leviticus 11; Deuteronomy 14).

- **v 21**

    Drinking wine.

3. **How does this help us to understand what Paul means by "weak" and "strong"?**

    A weak Christian is one who has not worked out the implications of the gospel on lifestyle and behavior. They are not those who have little faith, or little commitment to living out their faith. (In fact, the weak are generally the most fervent in trying to please God.) Their "weakness" is that they still live legalistically in some areas, and have not thought through how being saved by grace alone applies in those parts of their lives. The "strong" Christian is one who has understood that they are free to do something, and that their salvation does not depend on dos and don'ts.

Explore More

- *Read 1 Corinthians 8:1-13. What was the issue among the Christians in Corinth?*

    Whether Christians could buy and eat meat that was left over after pagan temple services.

- *What were the "weak" worried about, and what did the "strong" understand?*

    The weak were concerned that in eating that meat, even in their own homes and totally separate from any pagan worship, they were worshiping idols. The strong knew that it was only meat—that idols weren't real, and eating meat did not mean you were coming under the power of the idol.

- ○ ***So how are the weak and the strong the other way around from in the Roman church?***

  The weak Christians in Corinth were those who had come out of a background of idol-worship, and now felt polluted when they had anything to do with them—Gentiles. The strong were likely mainly Jewish Christians, who had no such history. In Rome, it was the other way around: the weak were those with a Jewish background, who were concerned about the Old Testament food laws; the strong were the Gentiles, who had no such anxieties.

  Setting these two passages alongside each other shows us that, with regard to a particular issue, one ethnic or social grouping could fall into being "weak," yet be "strong" in another area. We are all very able to be weak or strong or both at the same time!

---

4. **How do the weak and the strong tend to view each other (v 3)?**

   The strong feel superior to the weak—they "look down on" them. The strong feel much more mature, advanced, wise, or spiritually sophisticated. They will naturally see the weak as being narrow-minded or simple. So when the weaker Christian tells the stronger believer that they have an issue with a behavior, they respond, "That's your problem!" They feel completely justified in proceeding with their practice, because they know that it is not forbidden by God.

   The weak will tend to "condemn the man who does" what they think to be wrong. They will denounce and warn the strong that they are in grave spiritual danger—that they are sinning. They may even judge that the strong are not actually Christians.

5. **What does Paul tell the weak that they are forgetting when they condemn a Christian who does something they consider forbidden?**

- **v 1b**

  They cannot distinguish between matters of basic principle and matters of conscience—"disputable matters." A matter of conscience is one where God has not clearly forbidden nor clearly commanded it.

- **v 3b**

  "God has accepted" the believer whom the weak condemn because of their behavior. Whatever a Christian's strength or weakness or views, they have been completely accepted by the Father through Christ. The weak need to accept their brother or sister, and not condemn them; God has not (8:1).

- **v 4**

  God is the one who judges (to judge here means condemn and denounce).

- **v 5-8**

  They have forgotten to think through their own position. They might be wrong! Verse 5 suggests they need first to think out their own position before rushing to judgment. And, if God has not spoken on this matter, then just as they are seeking to please and thank God in how they live, so is the person they are disagreeing with (v 6). All belong to the Lord (v 7-8).

- **v 10-12**

    All of us will have to answer for our own conduct when we meet God (v 12); so rather than focusing on what another Christian is doing, we should make sure we are educating our own consciences with Scripture, and then live by them.

    To summarize: weak Christians are forgetting that Christians must accept anyone the Lord has accepted; not condemn anyone he has not condemned; and ensure they themselves have consciences that are in line with the gospel, and are living that out.

6. If and when we find ourselves judging another Christian's behavior, what has Paul taught us to think and do?

- God has accepted and welcomed this person, in Christ, as his child; I must treat them as a brother.
- God does not condemn this person; neither must I.
- Am I actually right to think that what they're doing is wrong? Is it actually a matter of Christian freedom? Am I elevating my personal preference to a matter of Christian principle? Am I being more black and white than God has been in his word?
- Am I living according to my own conscience?
- NOTE: This is not to say that a Christian will never warn a fellow believer about their behavior in these disputable matters. In fact, if they are convinced that Scripture says an action is sinful, the loving thing is to confront a believer who is behaving that way (12:9-10). But we will not judge or condemn each other; and we will check our own position, and our own lifestyle, first.

7. What should the priority of a strong believer be (v 13)?

Not to put any stumbling block or obstacle in another Christian's path. "Stumble" does not mean "bother," but rather, to cause someone to "fall" (v 21)—to retard or thwart another Christian's growth or relationship with Christ.

8. Why not (v 14-21)?

Trace Paul's argument through these verses:

- v 14: If someone thinks something is wrong, then it is wrong for them to do it (even if it is, in fact, not wrong) (v 14).
- NOTE: For why unclean foods are now permitted, turn to Jesus' words in Mark 7:14-15 and God's word to Peter in Acts 10:15, 28.
- v 15: If they indulge their freedom to eat meat when they are with a believer who thinks that is wrong, then first they are not being loving—they are doing something that will grieve someone else—and second, the

work of God is being destroyed—they are slowing a brother or sister's growth into maturity.
- v 16: They are giving an opportunity for a freedom—something God thinks good—to be seen as wrong, or evil.
- v 17-18: They are forgetting what is really important in the Christian life (as is the weaker Christian). Their behavior is being guided by their desire to eat meat, rather than their desire to promote "righteousness, peace and joy in the Holy Spirit" (v 17), which pleases God (v 18). (Ironically, both the weak and the strong Christian are making far too much of eating meat, and forgetting what really matters.)
- v 19-21: Paul recapitulates his argument. Peace and benefitting other believers is to drive our behavior, rather than enjoying our freedoms. In fact (v 20) to cause someone to stumble is "wrong" even if the action that causes it is not wrong.

9. **What would be the problem with that Christian acting in that way, even though it is not wrong?**
Because they are doing what they think is wrong, and not what they think faithfulness to God involves. So they are choosing something (their pleasure or pleasing others, and so on) over being faithful to God. That is sin. It is right to encourage a weaker Christian to educate their conscience; but we must not cause them to injure their conscience.

10. **How does 15:1 sum up what a strong Christian's priority should be?**
Positively, to use their strength to bear with the weak—to do what is best for those who are weaker. Negatively, not to please themselves—not to do what is easiest or most pleasant for themselves.

NOTE: Paul continues with his thought in verse 2 and uses the word "neighbor," which means he is extending the teaching beyond relationships within churches. We will look more at this in the next study.

11. **If and when another Christian thinks of as wrong something that we know we are free to do, what has Paul taught us to think and do?**
- Gently encourage them to think about whether or not Scripture really forbids what they are calling wrong.
- Refrain from behaving in that way while we are with them, or when they might hear of it (or, perhaps, completely), in order to make sure that they are not tempted to do what they believe is wrong.

12. **What are the "disputable matters" in your church, where Paul's words here need to be applied, whether we're "weak" or "strong"?**
NOTE: Some people tend to want to put everything in the "disputable matters" category, when clearly some issues are not for dispute (e.g. the identity of Christ, how we are saved, moral issues about which God has spoken clearly in his word). Others tend to want to put nothing

in the disputable matters category, making every single item of doctrine and behavior into a virtual salvation issue (e.g. baptism; how Christians should court/date; church government). The matters that are disputable and that we disagree over will vary from church to church and culture to culture. Others could include styles of music, drinking alcohol, and wearing makeup.

- **How could the weak and strong get it wrong in those areas?**

  This is an opportunity for you to finish the study by thinking about the pitfalls in those areas you have identified. Be careful not to speak in a condemnatory or critical way as you discuss them!

7

Ministry and Mission

Romans 15 - 16

The Big Idea
Effective gospel ministry springs from the motive of using all you have to serve others. It is Bible-centered, fosters true unity, is evangelistic and deed-based, and uses everyone's gifts; and its aim is to share the gospel and establish people in the gospel.

Summary
This study brings us to the end of Romans. And it presents us with a picture of what gospel ministry in a local church (and other forms of ministry) will look like. Paul shows us, in his encouragements to the Romans and his account of his own ministry, that gospel ministry produces churches where…

- people use their abilities and strengths to serve others, rather than please themselves (15:1-3).
- the Scriptures are read and taught as words for today, to encourage and give enduring hope (v 4).
- there is a deep, Spirit-given, barrier-breaking unity, based on following Christ together (v 5-13).
- evangelism is held as a central aspect of the Christian life, prompted by gratitude to God, and aiming to produce lifelong disciples (v 16-24).
- deed ministry (social help) is seen as an important response to what God has done (v 25-29).
- prayer for others is regular and heartfelt (v 30-33).

- every member contributes to the ministry in different ways (16:1-16).
- the church membership is diverse, drawn from both sexes, all backgrounds, and all levels of society and wealth (16:1-16).

Paul finishes with a great passage of praise and prayer to God (v 25-27), which picks up many of the themes of the letter. He points us back to the gospel, which underpins his life and his teaching—the gospel that was promised, was revealed in Christ, and is powerful to save and keep God's people, to the glory of God.

Optional Extra

The letter to the Roman church was written to be read aloud, in one go (rather than being read privately, in small chunks). So, having finished studying through all (or the second half) of Romans, read through it all, aloud. You could choose to read it all yourself, or ask a member of your group to (especially if they are stage-trained); or each read a chapter, until all 16 have been read. When you reach the end of the letter, have a time of open prayer.

Guidance for Questions

1. What do you think effective gospel ministry involves?

Here, there is no right answer and no single answer. Let your group discuss the various areas of good gospel-based ministry. Encourage them to see that they could all say different things and all be right, because gospel ministry is not only preaching, or evangelism, or doing good practically, and so on.

2. What ethical principle is laid down in verses 1-2?

The people with the power must be stewards of their power to build up and please those who are weak. They are not to use their power to build themselves up and make themselves comfortable. Notice that Paul uses the word "neighbor" in verse 2—while only Christians are my brothers and sisters, any human being is my "neighbor" (Luke 10:25-37). So in whatever way we are "strong" (economic, cultural, social and so on), we are to use that strength to serve others.

- **In what way is Jesus the great example of living this way (v 3)?**

He was the most powerful, strongest man who ever lived; yet he used all he was and had in the service of others. He never "pleased himself." Paul quotes from Psalm 69, where a good and righteous man endures undeserved suffering and persecution because he serves God. Paul is saying that Jesus was willing to be mocked, tortured, and killed by those who are God's enemies—and he did all that to serve those around him. We are to have that same attitude toward everyone around us—to live sacrificially to build them up.

3. **What do verses 3-4 teach us about the role that Scripture should have in our lives and churches?**
   - The Scriptures are entirely applicable to today: each part was "written to teach us." Anything preserved in the Bible is preserved to teach us something. Every part has lessons and applications.
   - The Scriptures are centered on Christ. Paul's ability to quote Psalm 69 and apply it to Christ reminds us that, basically, all of Scripture is about Jesus. He himself told two of his followers on the day he rose from the dead that "all the Scriptures" were about him (Luke 24:27).
   - The Scriptures, when read and heard with faith, increase "hope" in us. They do this through helping us endure (they are very realistic, and they call us to hard work and discipline—to keep going), and through encouragement (the Bible makes wonderful, precious promises). If we are willing to listen both to its commands and its promises, the Bible increases joyful persistence in life—hope.

4. **In verses 5-13, Paul is talking about the unique unity churches have. What do verses 5-7 tell us about how Christian unity is formed?**
   - v 5a: It is a supernatural gift from God. No method can create it—God gives it.
   - v 5b: It comes "as you follow Christ." This unity does not come by seeking it directly, as an end in itself. Rather, it is a by-product of seeking something else: namely, following Christ. It is as we commit to following Christ that we experience deep unity with those who have the same commitment.
   - v 6: It is as we worship "with one heart and mouth" that unity is enhanced. God gives spiritual unity so that we can worship together ("one heart and mouth" requires that we are united!); so committing to worshiping together will foster our unity.
   - v 7: It is based on our justification in Christ. We accept each other on the same basis that Christ has accepted us—we are loved by him despite all our flaws, so we love others despite theirs.

5. **How might the principle of verses 1-2 apply to your...**
- **finances?**

   Christians with money are to look at their money as given to them by God in order that they can use it to enrich and lift up those without it.

- **relationships?**

   We are not simply to relate to "our own kind," or work at good relationships only with those who benefit us or build us up emotionally. We must be willing to love and relate to people who are draining or difficult.

- **choice of where to live?**

   Instead of asking, "Where would I be most comfortable living?" we should ask, "Where can I live to be most useful, to God and to others?"

- OPTIONAL: **What would you have done differently in the past if you'd taken Romans 15:1-2 as the basis for how you made each decision? How might you think differently about decisions you are facing now or will face in the near future?**

  Depending on how comfortable your group are with being open with each other, you could ask them to think about this quietly, or to discuss and share their reflections.

6. What do we learn about Paul's ministry of evangelism here?

For each of the bullet points below, you could point your group to the verses highlighted and turn each point into a question (e.g. for Paul's motives: "What do verses 16-17 tell us about Paul's motive for evangelism?").

- *Motive (v 16-17)*: When Paul talks about his evangelism being a "priestly duty" with the goal of the Gentiles becoming "an offering acceptable to God," he is saying that those who are converted by his witness are his offering to God. He evangelizes as a way of giving God praise and thanks.
- *Aim (v 18)*: "Leading the Gentiles to obey God." What Paul wants is for people to come to real faith, which leads to sacrificial obedience (1:5; 12:1). He is not trying to produce some kind of "conversion experience," but completely changed lives. His evangelism aims to produce disciples.
- *Importance (v 18)*: Paul will not "speak of anything except what Christ has accomplished through me in leading the Gentiles to obey God." This is a strong statement! Paul accomplished many things (he was probably the greatest theologian in the history of the church); but the thing that drove him and excited him was the people whom he was seeing pass from death to life under his ministry.
- *Means (v 18)*: "By what I have said and done." Paul not only got the gospel message across by speaking but by his life and actions. He was able to show people the gospel as well as tell people the gospel; people could look at his life and see what it means to have your life rearranged by the gospel. (You may like at this point to move forward to the Explore More, which underlines this point, before returning to the rest of this question).
- NOTE: Paul mentions "signs and miracles" (v 19). Should we expect to do the same today? This is a large subject, but likely Paul's signs were part of his commission as an apostle (see 2 Corinthians 12:12). God can perform miracles today; but we should not expect him to do so (or, worse, demand that he do so). Nevertheless, we should make sure that our deeds are witnessing, just as our words are.

- *Strategy (v 20, 23).* Paul was a "pioneer"; his passion was to go into places where no one had heard the gospel, rather than build on someone else's work. And verse 23 suggests that he focused on urban areas (as Acts makes clear); so he is saying that in the area in question (v 19), he has planted churches in urban areas that previously had none, and so his part of the work is completed.

- **What applies to all Christians today, do you think?**

The motive and the aim can serve as ideals for all Christians.

Many of us simply don't have a passion for evangelism—we need to reflect on our own salvation so that a deep desire to serve and praise God is stirred up, and to see our evangelism as part of that. And we need to make sure we are aiming at producing disciples rather than just professions of faith (which can lead us to be superficial and short-term in our evangelism). But we are not all called to make evangelism the central purpose of our lives; nor to be an urban pioneering evangelist.

However, Paul's example should make the church as a whole recognize the importance of those who are called to this kind of mission, and the importance of praying for and supporting them.

Explore More

○ **Read 1 Thessalonians 2:1-12. From this passage, what does effective evangelism and church leadership involve?**

Sharing your whole life with people. Paul's love meant that he did share the gospel in Thessalonica, but that he not only shared the gospel; he also shared his whole life (v 8). And notice that his evangelism involved pastoring the new Christians too (v 9, 11-12). All this is very sacrificial and involves hard work (v 9).

○ **What motivates this kind of whole-life, sacrificial ministry (v 4, 6)?**

Pleasing God, rather than seeking popularity among people. This reminds us that Paul's evangelism was part of his life offered as a "living sacrifice" (Romans 12:1); it was his response to God's mercy to him, done in order to please his Lord.

7. **Paul was called to be a church-planting missionary. Why is it striking that he found time to raise money for, and deliver money to, the poverty-stricken churches around Jerusalem?**

Because it shows how important practical ministry is. Refer back to verses 23-24—Paul wants to go via Rome to Spain to preach there, but he is interrupting his evangelistic plans to collect and deliver this offering to Judea.

- **How does Paul motivate the Roman Christians to give?**

  Not by explaining the circumstances of the poverty, or the plight of the Jerusalem Christians. Rather, through pointing out the example of others (v 26) and the fact that they "owe" those who need help (v 27). Helping the poor is not an option, but a necessity—a duty.

  NOTE: Here, there is a special "owing" because the poor Christians are Jews, through whom the gospel has reached out to Gentiles such as the Christians in Rome. But 2 Corinthians 8:8-9 makes clear that wealthier Christians should give to poorer believers because they live out of gratitude for what Christ gave up in order to give to them.

  In Romans 15:26, Paul adds that Christians are "pleased" to give. It is a duty, but it brings pleasure. His point is that if our hearts are full of gratitude for God's sacrifice and grace, and love for fellow believers, then we will be pleased to give graciously and sacrificially to others. Christians don't give merely because they are required to but because they want to, and are joyful in that.

8. **How can the Christians in Rome join Paul in his struggles (v 30)? Why is this exciting?**

   By praying. This is exciting because it means we can always help a struggling brother or sister, by praying. We can come alongside those laboring many miles away, whom we may never have met, by praying for them. There is no struggle we cannot enter into and help someone through, because we can pray.

9. **Verses 1-23 give us some glimpses into the life of the early churches. What do they suggest to us about…**

- **the ministry of women?**

  Phoebe (v 1-2) is described as a "servant" or "deaconess" (see NIV footnote) i.e. ministry-server. We're not told exactly what role Phoebe had in the church, but she had used it to be of "great help," so that she was commended by an apostle. Women were clearly prominent and important in the early church.

- **the diversity of the church?**

  (You may need to help your group here.) The names suggest both Jews (v 7) and Gentiles: some of high rank (Aristobulus, v 10; Narcissus, v 12). There are men and women involved in ministry. This was a mixed church in many ways.

- **the structure of the church?**

  It was essentially a series of house churches (v 5).

- **the dangers to the church?**

  There was always the potential for false teaching to lead the church astray from apostolic truth (v 17). People with motives very different than Paul's could influence these Christians (v 18). There was a need always to be on guard against such people and such teachings (v 19).

10. **From these two chapters, what are the various ministries a church should be involved in?**

    Bible teaching (15:3-4); fellowship (v 5-6); evangelism (v 14-23); practical and financial support (v 25-29); all members using their gifts, houses, etc. (16:1-16).

- **Evaluate your own congregation and yourself individually in light of what you've seen.**

    Aim to keep this discussion positive. What can you start doing better, or more, or for the first time?

11. **These are the final words of this wonderful letter. How do they sum up several of its main themes?**
    - *What the gospel does*—"is able to" comes from the same Greek word as "is powerful to." (You will likely need to tell your group this!) So 16:25 links back to 1:16; the gospel is how God changes people and keeps his people. Paul is looking back to chapters 1 – 5: why we need the gospel and how the gospel saves us; and to chapters 6 – 8: how the gospel changes us.
    - *What the gospel is*—it is the proclamation of Jesus Christ" (16:25). See 1:3-4: "The gospel is "regarding his Son … Jesus Christ our Lord." The center of the gospel is Jesus, the divine man who died and rose to rule.
    - *Where the gospel is*—it was promised in "the prophetic writings," but only fully "revealed" in Christ (16:26-27; see 1:2; 3:21).
    - *What the gospel does (again)*—it is for all nations, to bring them to "believe and obey" God (16:26; see 1:5), to bring glory to God (16:27).

12. **Think back over your time in Romans 8 – 16 over the last seven sessions. Pick one encouragement the Lord has been giving you as an individual, and to your church, through this part of his word.**

- **Pick one challenge you feel the Lord has been posing you, and your church.**

    Give your group time to write in their own answers here, and then share them and talk them through.

Go Deeper with the Expository Guides to
Romans
by Timothy Keller

Less academic than a traditional commentary, these expository guides by Timothy Keller take you through the entire book of Romans, showing how the gospel in your heart can change you in a profound way.

These flexible resources can enrich your personal devotions, help you lead small-group studies, or aid your sermon preparations.

Explore the God's Word For You series

thegoodbook.com/for-you
thegoodbook.co.uk/for-you
thegoodbook.com.au/for-you

Bible-Study Guide to
Romans 1-7
by Timothy Keller

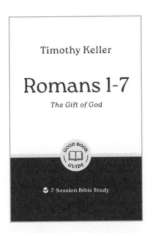

This seven-session Bible study on Romans 1 - 7 by Timothy Keller will help you understand one of the most read, most written-about parts of the Bible.

Each of the seven sessions has a simple, easy-to-follow structure with carefully crafted questions that help you look closely at the Bible text and apply it meaningfully to your everyday life. There is also a concise Leader's Guide at the back.

Explore the whole range of Good Book Guides

 thegoodbook.com/gbgs
thegoodbook.co.uk/gbgs
thegoodbook.com.au/gbgs

Explore the Whole Range

Old Testament, including:

  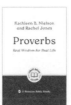 

New Testament, including:

   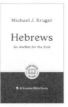

Topical, including:

Flexible and easy to use, with over 50 titles available, Good Book Guides are perfect for both groups and individuals.

thegoodbook.com/gbgs
thegoodbook.co.uk/gbgs
thegoodbook.com.au/gbgs

God's Word For You

Accessible Commentaries That Everyone Can Enjoy

Old Testament, including:

New Testament, including:

Less academic than a traditional commentary, these expository guides take you verse by verse through books of the Bible in an accessible, applied way. These flexible resources can enrich your personal devotions, help you lead small-group studies, or aid your sermon preparations.

Use with accompanying Good Book Guides to study these books of the Bible in small groups.

thegoodbook.com/for-you
thegoodbook.co.uk/for-you
thegoodbook.com.au/for-you

BIBLICAL | RELEVANT | ACCESSIBLE

At The Good Book Company we are dedicated to helping Christians and local churches grow. We believe that God's growth process always starts with hearing clearly what he has said to us through his timeless and flawless word—the Bible.

Ever since we opened our doors in 1991, we have been striving to produce resources that are biblical, relevant, and accessible. By God's grace, we have grown to become an international publisher, encouraging ordinary Christians of every age and stage and every background and denomination to live for Christ day by day and equipping churches to grow in their knowledge of God, their love for one another, and the effectiveness of their outreach.

Call one of our friendly team for a discussion of your needs or visit one of our local websites for more information on the resources and services we provide.

Your friends at The Good Book Company

thegoodbook.com | thegoodbook.co.uk
thegoodbook.com.au | thegoodbook.co.nz